A History of Entrepreneurship

This book establishes a chronological trace of the entrepreneur as treated in economic literature in order to give a more illuminating perspective to contemporary writings and teachings on entrepreneurship. It focuses on the nature and role of the entrepreneur and of entrepreneurship as revealed in economic literature as early as the eighteenth century, when Richard Cantillon first coined the term "entrepreneur". The authors then trace how Joseph Schumpeter's perspective, among others, on entrepreneurship came to dominate the world's understanding of the term.

Due to Schumpeter's dominant influence, entrepreneurship has come to occupy a primary role in the theory of economic development. In this book Hébert and Link discuss various key topics, including the German tradition, the Austrian and the English School of thought, and individuals such as Alfred Marshall and Jeremy Bentham. The historical survey also illustrates the tension that often exists between "theory" and "practice" and how it has been difficult for economic theory to assimilate a core concept that plays a vital role in social and economic change. Finally, the book exposes the many different facets of entrepreneurship as they have been perceived by some of the great economists throughout the ages.

This fascinating and insightful book will be of interest to students and researchers in the history of economic thought as well as thoughtful scholars of entrepreneurship everywhere.

Robert F. Hébert is Russell Professor of Economics, Emeritus, at Auburn University, U.S.A.

Albert N. Link is Professor of Economics at the University of North Carolina at Greensboro, U.S.A.

Routledge Studies in the History of Economics

A History of Entrepreneurship

**Robert F. Hébert
and Albert N. Link**

Routledge
Taylor & Francis Group

LONDON AND NEW YORK

First published 2009
by Routledge
2 Park Square, Milton Park, Abingdon, Oxon, OX14 4RN

Simultaneously published in the USA and Canada
by Routledge
270 Madison Avenue, New York, NY 10016

Routledge is an imprint of the Taylor & Francis Group, an informa business

© 2009 Robert F. Hébert and Albert N. Link

Reprinted 2009, 2010

Typeset in Times New Roman by Pindar NZ, Auckland, New Zealand

British Library Cataloging in Publication Data
A catalog record for this book is available from the British Library

Library of Congress Cataloging-in-Publication Data
Hébert, Robert F.
A history of entrepreneurship / Robert F. Hébert and Albert N. Link.
   p. cm.
   Includes bibliographical references and index.
   1. Entrepreneurship—History. 2. Entrepreneurship—Cross-
cultural studies. 3. Business people. I. Link, Albert N. II. Title.
   HB615.H342 2009
   338'.0409—dc22   2008049347

ISBN10: 0-415-77738-0 (hbk)
ISBN10: 0-203-87732-2 (ebk)

ISBN13: 978-0-415-77738-4 (hbk)
ISBN13: 978-0-203-87732-6 (ebk)

\# 276274621

Contents

About the authors

Robert F. Hébert is Emeritus Russell Foundation Professor of Entrepreneurial Studies at Auburn University. He received his doctorate from Louisiana State University in Baton Rouge in 1970. His teaching career included stints at Louisiana State University, Clemson University, Auburn University, the University of Louisiana at Lafayette, the University of Paris (Sorbonne), and the Institut d'Administration des Entreprises de Caen. In 1994–95 he was Fulbright Senior Research Scholar in France. He is a past trustee of the Southern Economics Association and past president of the History of Economics Society. His research is centered on the history of economic thought, economic history, and, most recently, the economics of religion. Professor Hébert's publications include articles in the *Journal of Political Economy*, *Economica*, the *Quarterly Journal of Economics*, and many others. His recent books include: *Secret Origins of Modern Microeconomics: Dupuit and the Engineers*, with R. B. Ekelund, Jr. (University of Chicago Press, 1999); *The Marketplace of Christianity*, with R. B. Ekelund, Jr. and R. D. Tollison (MIT Press, 2006); and *A History of Economic Theory and Method*, fifth edition, with R. B. Ekelund, Jr. (Waveland Press, 2007). Currently Professor Hébert is retired and living in Baton Rouge, Louisiana.

Albert N. Link is Professor of Economics at the University of North Carolina at Greensboro. He received a B.S. degree in mathematics from the University of Richmond and a Ph.D. degree in economics from Tulane University. His research focuses on innovation policy, university entrepreneurship, and the economics of research and development. He is the Editor-in-Chief of the *Journal of Technology Transfer*. Professor Link's research has appeared in such journals as the *American Economic Review*, the *Journal of Political Economy*, the *Review of Economics and Statistics*, and *Economica*. His most recent books include: *Government as Entrepreneur* (Oxford University Press, 2009); *The Economics of*

Innovation Policy (Edward Elgar, 2008); *The Economic Theory of Invention and Innovation* (Edward Elgar, 2008); *Innovation, Entrepreneurship, and Technological Change* (Oxford University Press, 2007); *Innovation in the U.S. Service Sector* (Routledge, 2006); and *Entrepreneurship and Technology Policy* (Edward Elgar, 2006). Much of Professor Link's research has been supported by the National Science Foundation, the OECD, the World Bank, and various science and technology ministries in developed nations. Currently, Professor Link is serving as the Vice-Chairperson of the Innovation and Competitiveness Policies Committee of the United Nations Economic Commission for Europe (UNECE).

Preface

For more than two and a half decades we have been writing about the entrepreneur: who he or she is and what he or she does. Our mission began when we both were on the faculty at Auburn University. Early on, we realized there were topics to be studied that married our respective interests – history of economic thought and innovation. Our first monograph on the subject of the entrepreneur, *The Entrepreneur: Mainstream Views and Radical Critiques*, appeared in 1982. It chronicled the nature of entrepreneurship as conceived by various writers throughout the history of economic thought, raising issues unresolved to this day. Six years later our work was expanded and reissued in a second edition.

Our effort was well received by economists who appreciated – and furthered – the role of the entrepreneur in economic theory. G. L. S. Shackle wrote: "The history of ideas concerning the nature of entrepreneurship and the qualities it demands has been told [by Hébert and Link] with concision, clarity, and style." Israel Kirzner added: "A pioneering – and first-rate – effort [by Hébert and Link] in a long-neglected field."

But enough was not enough. Nearly twenty years after the publication of the second edition, we decided to revisit the subject in two academic journal articles in order to assess interim progress on the nature of entrepreneurship. These papers appeared in 2006 in the *Journal of Technology Transfer* and in *Foundation and Trends in Entrepreneurship*. This book finalizes our disquisition on the historical nature of entrepreneurship and affords some reflection on the subject moving forward. The most basic questions persist on the entrepreneur (e.g., who he or she is) and entrepreneurship (e.g., what he or she does). Thus the challenge of pinpointing and refining the essence of entrepreneurship is as vigorous today as it was when we first took up the subject more than twenty years ago.

Our motivation for revisiting this subject now is twofold. First, from a pragmatic perspective, this book affords an opportunity for us to synthesize our twenty-five-plus years of thought on the subject. And second, the explosion of interest in the academic field of entrepreneurship and the proliferation of undergraduate and graduate courses on the topic has occurred almost completely out of touch with the historical evolution of the concept. Recent advances in the mathematical nature of economics have often come at the expense of historical perspectives that provide an important touchstone to the reality of human events. Hopefully this book will provide a useful resource to younger scholars to keep them grounded in the historical aspects of economic theory.

Throughout our academic careers, our wives – Diane and Carol – have unselfishly provided support and inspiration. We dedicate this book to them in modest repayment for their love and understanding.

Introduction

Throughout intellectual history the prominence of the entrepreneur and his or her role in economic theory has been intertwined with dynamic versus static representations of economic activity. The science of economics – which began as "political economy" in the eighteenth century – was initially concerned with a dynamic problem, namely the explanation of how economic progress occurs. Hence we have Adam Smith's telling title of his masterwork, *An Inquiry into the Nature and Causes of the Wealth of Nations*, written in 1776. During the infancy of economic science, the entrepreneur emerged as an economic agent central to the operation of product and resource markets. Progress in defining and explaining the entrepreneur and his role was halting at first; indeed the best work in this regard was done before Smith, who obscured the issue somewhat by confounding the roles of entrepreneur and capitalist. Karl Marx continued the classical tradition of inquiry into the dynamics of capitalism, but because he treated capitalist and entrepreneur alike with disdain, the concept of entrepreneurship languished thereafter.

After roughly a century of development, conventional economics rejected Marx's radicalism and reinvented itself as the science of how scarce resources are allocated in an efficient manner, a problem largely static in nature. For several succeeding generations the role of the entrepreneur was neglected as economists labored to refine and extend economic theory within an equilibrium framework. During this time entrepreneurship became the province of sociology, which, among other things, concerned itself with the nature and character of leadership. The entrepreneur remained prominent in economics but only to the extent that the area of investigation was economic development.

In the twentieth century the name more closely associated with entrepreneurship above all others was Joseph Schumpeter, who constructed *The Theory of Economic Development* (1912) around the dynamic, innovative actions of the equilibrium-disturbing entrepreneur. This gave rise to the phrase "Schumpeterian entrepreneur," which tacitly suggests that there are other kinds of entrepreneurs who conceivably do different things. Yet there have been few inquiries to determine what those other things are and which economic agent is responsible for them.

Eventually the entrepreneur attracted the attention of management, which was forced to ferret out the distinctions between entrepreneurs and managers. As a result, entrepreneurship is a focal point today for at least three disciplines – economics, sociology, and management – and it could become prominent in even more (e.g., psychology). It might be expected that this multi-pronged approach to the study of entrepreneurship would resolve key issues such as "Who is the entrepreneur?", "What is the key function of the entrepreneur in a market economy?", and thus "What is entrepreneurship?" No such consensus has emerged, however.

The fractured nature of entrepreneurship is a striking anomaly that accompanies dramatic growth of interest in the subject, both academic and practical. Joseph Schumpeter began teaching at Harvard University in 1932. In conjunction with Arthur Cole, he started the Research Center in Entrepreneurial History in 1946. The following year Myles Mace offered what may be the first U.S. course on entrepreneurship to 188 students at the Harvard Business School (Katz 2003). Since then, the growth of entrepreneurship in higher education has been remarkable. By the dawn of the twenty-first century, nearly 200,000 American students had been enrolled in entrepreneurship or small business courses. Currently there are more than 2,200 courses on the subject at more than 1,600 colleges and universities (Katz 2003). In addition, there are more than 150 university research centers on entrepreneurship, according to the Global Consortium of Entrepreneurship Centers.[1]

Informed speculation says that the demand for entrepreneurship education will outpace the supply of well-trained university faculty. Enrollments in entrepreneurship courses are increasing not only from traditional business and economics students but also from students in the fields of science and engineering.[2] In addition, the breadth of subject matter that now falls under the rubric of entrepreneurship is expanding.[3] It is not uncommon for courses on business entrepreneurship to include discussions of social entrepreneurship, political entrepreneurship, and academic entrepreneurship.

On the supply side, a shortage of qualified faculty is exacerbated by a dearth of doctoral programs in entrepreneurship (Katz 2003). In order to meet the excess demand for entrepreneurship education, many institutions are recruiting new business and management faculty and/or adjunct professors to teach the subject, usually with a specialized small-business focus. The instructors who fill the ranks often come from business rather than academe. The ensuing instruction tends to emphasize "hands-on" business practices and concrete problems, not conceptual issues or historical precedents. As a consequence, intellectual history of entrepreneurship is sacrificed to the pressing demands of the here and now; or it becomes merely one more victim of a pervasive anti-historical bias. If this trend continues, it is likely that all historical perspective on the subject of the entrepreneur will be lost.[4]

We have written this book in hopes of preserving a vital historical perspective. Our exposition derives from an economic point of view (not from sociology or management), and therefore it makes no claims to being holistic in its approach. This book establishes a chronological trace of the entrepreneur as treated in economic literature in order to give a more wholesome perspective to contemporary writings and teachings on entrepreneurship. In the following chapters we review the historical nature and role of the entrepreneur, and thus of entrepreneurship, as revealed in economic literature from the eighteenth century to the present.[5] This kind of survey is instructive in several ways. It shows, for example, the ambiguous nature of a concept that, due to Schumpeter's dominant influence, has come to occupy a primary role in the theory of economic development. We shall learn that there are other conceptions of entrepreneurship besides Schumpeter's. Indeed, throughout history the entrepreneur has worn many faces and played many roles. Our historical survey also illustrates the tension that often exists between "theory" and "practice." We shall learn that it has been difficult for economic theory to assimilate a core concept that plays a vital role in social and economic change. Finally, our historical survey will expose the many different facets of entrepreneurship as they have been perceived by some of the great economists throughout the ages.

The historical economics literature gives no fewer than twelve identities to the entrepreneur. We shall explore at length each of these identities in the remainder of this book. But first we expose the various themes we shall encounter.

1   The entrepreneur is the person who assumes the risk associated with uncertainty.
2   The entrepreneur is the person who supplies financial capital.
3   The entrepreneur is an innovator.
4   The entrepreneur is a decision-maker.
5   The entrepreneur is an industrial leader.
6   The entrepreneur is a manager or superintendent.
7   The entrepreneur is an organizer and coordinator of economic resources.
8   The entrepreneur is the owner of an enterprise.
9   The entrepreneur is an employer of factors of production.
10 The entrepreneur is a contractor.
11 The entrepreneur is an arbitrageur.
12 The entrepreneur is an allocator of resources among alternative uses.

Already it will be obvious that considerable overlap exists. Some writers stressed more than one characteristic. Some views are competing; some are complementary. The entrepreneur, in sum, is a difficult person to pin down; entrepreneurship, in sum, is a difficult activity or mindset to pin down. Nevertheless, when we contemplate this list we are struck by the preponderance of emphasis on the entrepreneur as a dynamic, not a passive, economic agent. The dynamism of economic agents is not a trivial matter. In a *Wall Street Journal* article entitled "Dynamic Capitalism" (October 10, 2006), Edmund S. Phelps, winner of the 2006 Nobel Prize in Economic Science, compared the two prevailing economic systems of the West, free enterprise versus corporatism. He concluded that only the former provides the openness, encouragement, and flexibility that permit greatest implementation of new commercial ideas coming from entrepreneurs. Phelps defines "dynamism" as meaning the fertility of the economy in coming up with innovative ideas believed to be technologically feasible and profitable – in short, the economy's talent at commercially successful innovating. Because competition is so closely linked to entrepreneurship, he might as easily have drawn the contrast between the "entrepreneurial economy" and the "corporate economy."

In looking outside the United States today (and even to some quarters within the United States), one encounters mostly hostility directed toward the kind of dynamic capitalism that Phelps extols. Why is capitalism so reviled in Western Europe, for example? The reasons are undoubtedly as convoluted as they are complicated, but one reason seems to be the inability of many intellectuals to escape Marxist patterns of thought. As Phelps points out, today's street protestors appear to equate business with established wealth, so they regard giving latitude to business as tantamount to increasing the privileges of old wealth and exacerbating disparity of incomes. By an "entrepreneur" such critics mean a rich owner of a bank or a factory, whereas for Schumpeter it meant a newcomer swimming against the tide of established wealth, seeking to carve out new profits from opportunities that did not exist before and, in the process, making consumers better off. Clearly, intellectual constructs matter in the battle of ideas taking place on the geopolitical stage. Is this not sufficient justification for investigation into the nature and role of the entrepreneur as revealed in the historical record?

1 The prehistory of entrepreneurship

The function, if not the name, of the entrepreneur is probably as old as the institutions of barter and exchange. But only after economic markets became an intrusive element of society did the concept take on pivotal importance. Many economists have recognized the pivotal role of the entrepreneur in a market economy. Yet despite his central importance in economic activity, the entrepreneur has been a shadowy and elusive figure in the history of economic theory.

Before research in entrepreneurship can be brought to a mature stage, we must be able to answer two simple yet critical questions: (1) Who is the entrepreneur? (2) What does he do that makes him unique? Regrettably, the answers to these questions are far from clear-cut. In modern economies, the distinction between entrepreneurial and non-entrepreneurial behavior is often blurred. And the history of the concept is not well understood or appreciated. As a result, there may be almost as many definitions of entrepreneurship as there are students of the subject. Joseph Schumpeter, in his compendious *History of Economic Analysis* (1954), traced the history of the subject at some length, but there is much of the story that he does not tell. Books and journal articles attack the issue piecemeal. The tendency of entrepreneurship to be dissected by different disciplines (e.g., economics, sociology, management) adds further to its fractional nature.

As previously mentioned, this book is delimited by its economic perspective. As an independent discipline, economics is hardly more than two centuries old. This makes it an elder statesman among the social sciences and business and management fields but a mere babe in the history of human activity. The font of information on the nature of entrepreneurship flowed well before Adam Smith gave form and structure to economics in 1776, but the most striking thing about this early period is the blankness of its record regarding the nature of entrepreneurship.

Merchants and adventurers

Early economic thought was sensitive to the fact that economic activity is human activity and that acting agents can roughly be divided into two classes: those who lead and those who follow. However ill-defined at present, entrepreneurial talent has always been closely aligned with the quality of leadership. Aside from royalty, the entrepreneur was typically found among the ranks of merchants or the military. Military leaders especially qualified, because wars were often fought for economic reasons. The general who designed and executed a successful strategy in battle took considerable risks and stood to gain substantial economic benefits.

Ancient merchants also subjected themselves and their possessions to risk in a way not unlike that of the military leader. Indeed, in early times the functions of trader and adventurer were often merged in the same individual. Marco Polo, for example, was an adventurer seeking to establish vital trade routes to the Orient, a land of many new and fascinating products. Even less peripatetic merchants were customarily exposed to many risks. Courage in business was not equated with courage in battle, however, and the merchant was held in low esteem by the ancient philosophers. Aristotle, for one, recognized the place of the merchant in society but did not regard him as having a high calling. On the contrary, he must be watched constantly lest society suffer from his overzealousness and rapaciousness. According to Aristotle (1924, p. 20) the act of moneymaking divides itself into household management and retail trade. He regarded the former as necessary and honorable, but he considered the latter unnatural because it provided a way for people to gain at the expense of another.

Of course the ancient Greek concern over maintenance of the status quo was partly a result of interpreting economic activity as a zero-sum game in which one person's gain was another person's loss – an idea whose dominance persisted into the eighteenth century. By this view, trade does nothing to enhance the aggregate well-being of society. Centuries of experience with markets should have taught us otherwise, but it is remarkable how stubbornly this idea persists in contemporary society. Profit, the return to successful entrepreneurship, remains suspect in the minds of many well-educated people today, partly because of a long Western tradition of equating businessman with bogeyman.

Early forms of business organization

The tendency to emphasize the importance of human decisions in the strategic nature of economic activity depends to a large extent on the kind of business organization that prevails.[1] In the ancient and medieval worlds,

trade took place on a relatively small scale; nevertheless, capital require-
ments were paramount. The link between the capitalist and the merchant
adventurer depended on the contract they signed. Beginning around 1000,
it became custom to lend money at 20 percent interest in contracts called
mutua, in which loans were tightly secured by real estate. In the late twelfth
century, the most common form of commercial investment was the sea
loan (*societas maris*), a cooperative agreement between a traveling and an
investing partner in which the interest paid was usually higher but the risks
of shipwreck and piracy were borne by the lender rather than the merchant.
According to Raymond de Roover (1963a), the traveling partner always
embarked on a hazardous sea voyage, handled the actual business, and risked
his life and limb but received only one-fourth of the profits, while the lion's
share of three-fourths went to the investing partner. By way of explanation,
de Roover (1963a, p. 49) remarked that the capitalist received a higher return
because "life was cheap and capital scarce."

In Venice, Europe's most active trading society in the thirteenth century,
the most prevalent contract was known as *colleganze* (elsewhere called
commende). By these contracts a capitalist could employ an agent by
promising him one-fourth of the profits, or an enterprising merchant could
mobilize the investments of several other people in his own hands. In the
fourteenth century, funds could be secured by merchants and adventurers
at terms dependent on the market rate of interest under a form of contract
known as the "local *colleganza*" (Lane 1963, p. 316). As trade expanded,
capital sometimes became concentrated in a full business partnership
(*compagnia*).

One expects that the cost of capital in such arrangements would reflect
the amount of risk incurred; and indeed, ancient trade documents generally
bear this out. However, Fritz Redlich (1966) found the explanation for high
returns to capital in the medieval prohibition against usury. The Church's
prohibition enjoined medieval businessmen from borrowing capital in
some loan markets and paying a fair rate of interest thereon. But certain
kinds of business contracts were exempt from the prohibition, including
the *colleganza* and the *societas maris*. Thus entrepreneurs were forced
by religious sanction to seek credit in arrangements approved (or at least
not forbidden) by the Church. The consequent restriction on the supply of
business capital could account for higher interest rates.

Economic writers during the Middle Ages were primarily theologians
writing under the auspices of the Church. De Roover (1963b, pp. 82–3)
claims that their consequent preoccupation with ethics seriously limited these
writers' interest in certain questions, among them entrepreneurship. Duns
Scotus and San Bernardino were exceptions. They agreed that merchants
were entitled to compensation for risk and recompense for their labor, albeit

in amounts limited by "justice." San Bernardino also stressed the qualities good merchants should possess: they must have good judgment with respect to risks; they must be well informed with respect to product qualities, prices and costs; they must be attentive to detail; and they must be prepared to suffer hardships and all manner of risks.

Property rights and the entrepreneurial function

Two main points may be gleaned from a review of ancient and medieval literature on entrepreneurship, sparse though it may be. First, the merchant-adventurer was a commonplace of ancient and medieval societies. Second, his success or lack of it depended on how well he fared in overcoming risk and/or legal and institutional constraints. Much of the remainder of this book deals with the relationship of risk to entrepreneurship. It is therefore incumbent upon us to say something about legal and institutional factors.

Entrepreneurs (whether ancient or modern) work within an institutional environment that itself often yields to entrepreneurial efforts. That is to say, there are "political entrepreneurs" who expend efforts to change institutional structures and practices in order to benefit themselves. Political entrepreneurship is not a major focus of this book; nevertheless, it is important to recognize at an early stage of inquiry the vital role of institutions in shaping entrepreneurial activities and rewards. This point is underscored by the following historical example.

An early manifestation of entrepreneurship involving risk-bearing and individual initiative existed in the medieval practice of tax farming. In medieval society, a tax farmer was one who successfully bid for the exclusive right to collect taxes in the name of the Crown. The amount of each bid is related in a predictable way to the bidder's evaluation of the amount of taxes he can collect. The advantage to the monarch who farms out the collection of taxes is that he knows his revenues and receives them in advance. The risk to the tax farmer is that he may collect less tax revenue than what he paid for the franchise to collect taxes. Of course if he collects more than the amount of his bid, he profits by the difference. The practice of tax farming can be traced back as far as ancient Greece and may, upon closer investigation, be found to be even older.

The practice of tax farming helps to explain how property rights ownership and the security of these rights impinge on the behavior of entrepreneurs. The incentive that spurs each entrepreneur to action is the opportunity to obtain profit. But making profit, while a necessary condition, is not a sufficient condition for entrepreneurial activity. The entrepreneur must also be reasonably assured that he can keep entrepreneurial profits that he acquires legitimately. Thus certain institutional practices in a market economy will tend to encourage a high level of entrepreneurial activity, especially (1) a free and open economy that permits equal access to entrepreneurial opportunities, (2) guarantees of ownership in property legally acquired, and (3) stability of institutional practices that establish both (1) and (2).

Perhaps the prevalence and longevity of tax farming as an entrepreneurial activity were due to the relatively greater security enjoyed by the fiscal entrepreneur as against the merchant-adventurer, whose goods were subject to fire, theft, storm, and other destruction and whose profit did not always reflect his diligence in supervision or management.

The evolution of a concept

Fritz Redlich (1966, p. 715) maintains, on the one hand, that in a business enterprise the provision of capital is on a par with management and strategic decision-making, for all three are necessary to business success. On the other hand, he says, "When we look at individual enterprises in specific situations any one of these three functions may temporarily become 'primary'." Something analogous can be said about the history of entrepreneurship. Over time, one aspect or another comprising "entrepreneurship" has vied for attention. Risk-bearing was among the earliest themes associated with entrepreneurship. But the risk-bearing function of entrepreneurship became less important after the establishment of new forms of business organization generated by the legal concept of limited liability. Subsequently, innovation came to be stressed over other aspects of entrepreneurship in theories of economic development. The third wave of entrepreneurial theories – one that still ripples through modern economic literature – stresses the importance of perception and adjustment in an equilibrating framework.

The term 'entrepreneur' does not appear often in the prehistory of economics. It is a word of French origin that enjoyed common, though imprecise, usage in the eighteenth century, as corroborated by *Savary's Dictionnaire Universel de Commerce* (1723), which defines an entrepreneur as one who undertakes a project; a manufacturer; a master builder. An earlier form of the word, *entreprendeur*, appears as early as the fourteenth century (Hoselitz 1960). Throughout the sixteenth and seventeenth centuries the most frequent usage of the term connoted a government contractor, usually of military fortifications or public works.

The typical entrepreneur of the Middle Ages, usually a cleric, was "the man in charge of the great architectural works: castles and fortifications, public buildings, abbeys and cathedrals" (Hoselitz 1960, p. 237). Until the end of the twelfth century, the functions of inventor, planner, architect, builder, manager, employer, and supervisor were all combined in the notion of an entrepreneur, but risk-bearing and capital provision were not part of the concept. As capitalism began to supplant feudalism, a clearer distinction emerged between the one who performed artistic and technical functions and the one who undertook the commercial aspects of a great task.

The first writer to narrow the meaning of the term, infuse it with precise economic content, and give it analytic prominence was Richard Cantillon, an eighteenth-century businessman and financier whose ideas on the subject are treated in the next chapter. Cantillon's work is a watershed in the development of entrepreneurial theory precisely because by the time we get to his treatment of the subject, emphasis is being placed squarely on the purely commercial aspects of getting things done in a market economy.

Postscript

From its inception the function of entrepreneurship has been intertwined with the availability of capital and the risk associated with commercial ventures. This nexus eventually led to the confounding of the roles of capitalist and entrepreneur, which in turn has led to retardation of full and unambiguous understanding of the nature of entrepreneurship. As a consequence, the concept of entrepreneur, as we shall see in ensuing sections of this book, was continuously reinvented to suit the purposes of individual economic writers. Moreover, it is difficult to have a proper appreciation of entrepreneurship without a thorough understanding of how markets function within a given set of property rights.

2   Early French contributions

The crucial role of the entrepreneur in economic theory was first and foremost recognized by Richard Cantillon (1680?–1734?), whose *Essai sur la Nature du Commerce en Général* was published posthumously in 1755, after circulating privately for two decades among a small group of French economists. Although several French writers borrowed freely from Cantillon's manuscript during its private circulation, it was relatively neglected after its publication until it was rediscovered in the nineteenth century by William Stanley Jevons, a pioneer in neoclassical economics. Today, Cantillon's *Essai* is rightfully considered a classic of early economic literature. Jevons enthusiastically called it "the cradle of political economy."

The details of Cantillon's life and activities are rather sparse. He was of Irish extraction, and he is often confused with a relative of the same name. The exact year of his birth has so far defied identification. Even the circumstances of his death are shrouded in mystery. He was a successful banker and financier, but controversy dogged him in everything. In Paris he made a fortune at the expense of John Law's infamous inflationary scheme known as the "Mississippi Bubble." Demonstrating considerable entrepreneurial skill in his own right, Cantillon anticipated the course of events set in motion by Law's "system" and profited handsomely from the financial opportunities that it presented.

In 1716 Law obtained permission from France's prince regent to establish a royal bank. Shortly thereafter he secured an exclusive franchise to form a trading company in the New World that was popularly known as the Mississippi Company. The company monopolized French foreign trade and eventually began to assume the French government's debt by trading shares of the company's stock for certificates of indebtedness. With the certificates came the exclusive right to collect certain taxes. Promises of large dividends to investors pushed share prices up sharply, and a frenzy of stock speculation ensued. The system came crashing down in 1720 when stock values rose out of proportion to the real value of the company's assets.

Cantillon made a great deal of money by liquidating his Mississippi Company holdings before the speculative boom peaked. With the proceeds of his own shares reinvested in Britain and Holland, he fed the British mania for speculation by advancing funds to English speculators who bought shares in the Mississippi Company that they subsequently pledged as collateral for their loans. Confident of the ultimate failure of Law's scheme, Cantillon sold the collateralized shares before the price of the stock broke, thus pocketing speculative profits in addition to the interest he collected on the loans he made. This practice provoked numerous lawsuits from his borrowers, but Cantillon successfully defended himself against their claims. This display of financial acumen stamped Cantillon as a successful entrepreneur in his own right, but his intellectual legacy was a greater testimony to his talents.

Entrepreneurs and markets

Cantillon's historic *Essai* sketched the outlines of a nascent market economy founded on individual property rights and based on economic interdependency, or what he called mutual "need and necessity." In this early market economy Cantillon recognized three classes of economic agents: (1) landowners, who are financially independent; (2) entrepreneurs, who engage in market exchanges at their own risk in order to make a profit; and (3) hirelings, who forego active decision-making in order to secure contractual guaranties of stable income (i.e., fixed wage contracts).

Cantillon depicts the landowners as the "fashion leaders" of the economy. By virtue of their wealth and social status, they establish patterns of consumption that conform to their individual tastes and preferences. It has been said that Cantillon placed the landowner at the top of his economic hierarchy, but a closer examination of his work reveals the entrepreneur as the central economic actor. Cantillon's *Essai* contains over a hundred references to the entrepreneur as a pivotal figure in the economic process. He laid it down as a general principle that entrepreneurs conduct all the production, circulation, and exchange in a market economy. As a motive force, entrepreneurs are much more important than the landowners, who collectively determine aggregate demand but otherwise retire to the sidelines of economic activity.

Cantillon's entrepreneur is someone who engages in exchanges for profit; specifically, he is someone who exercises business judgment in the face of uncertainty. This uncertainty (of future sales prices for goods on their way to final consumption) is rather carefully circumscribed. As Cantillon describes it, entrepreneurs buy at a certain price to sell again at an uncertain price, with the difference being their profit or loss.

The chief producers in Cantillon's day were farmers. "The farmer," Cantillon wrote, "is an entrepreneur who promises to pay to the landowner, for his farm or land, a fixed sum of money without assurance of the profit he will derive from this enterprise." As an entrepreneur-producer, the farmer decides how to allocate his land among various uses "without being able to foresee which of these will pay best." He must contend with the vagaries of weather and demand, placing himself at risk. Cantillon wrote that no one "can foresee the number of births and deaths of the people in a state in the course of the year," or the rise and decline of family spending, "and yet the price of the farmer's produce depends naturally upon these unforeseen circumstances, and consequently he conducts the enterprise of his farm at an uncertainty" (1931, pp. 47–9). Thus we have an explicit link between entrepreneurship and uncertainty.

In a market economy, the farmer is linked to consumers by other economic agents who also face uncertain incomes. Goods are usually distributed by middlemen who are intermediaries between producers and consumers. To the extent that these intermediaries face uncertainty in the marketplace, they too are entrepreneurs. These middlemen find markets for their services mainly in the cities. Cantillon (1931, p. 49) observed that more than half of farm output is consumed in the cities, where entrepreneurs set up shop to receive goods from the farms and to resell to ultimate consumers. The carriers and the wholesalers, through whose hands goods pass as they move from the farm to the customer, are also put at risk because of daily price fluctuations in the city. Time is the handmaiden of uncertainty.

The city creates opportunities for other entrepreneurs who are residents and who are willing to take risks in order to make goods available at the appropriate time and place. Each represents a link in the chain of distribution. Thus entrepreneurs who carry goods to the city usually sell to wholesalers, who subsequently sell at retail to ultimate consumers. In this manner, part of the risk is shifted from carriers to wholesalers and from wholesalers to retailers, each of whom provides time and place utility to consumers.

As markets develop, self-interested entrepreneurs spring up everywhere, goaded on by the lure of profit and joined together by mutual need or reciprocity. These entrepreneurs are encouraged because they know that consumers are willing to pay a little extra in order to buy in small quantities, when it is convenient, rather than bear the inconvenience and expense of stockpiling large quantities for their ultimate use (Cantillon 1931, pp. 51–3).

Cantillon broke with convention in emphasizing the economic function of the entrepreneur over his social status. Social standing is practically irrelevant to Cantillon's notion of entrepreneurship. The ranks of entrepreneurs are filled with people from all social strata. He went so far as to identify even beggars and robbers as entrepreneurs, provided they take chances (i.e., face economic uncertainty). Yet being an entrepreneur does not exclude one from being something else. Entrepreneurs and non-entrepreneurs alike are joined in reciprocal trade agreements with other market participants, such that they "become consumers and customers one in regard to the other," and proportion themselves to their customers in accordance with the laws of supply and demand. Like every other market, the market for entrepreneurs will adjust to market circumstances. "If there are too many hatters," Cantillon wrote, "for the number of people who buy hats … some who are least patronized must become bankrupt." Whereas, "If they be too few it will be a profitable undertaking which will encourage new hatters to open shops … so it is that the entrepreneurs of all kinds adjust themselves to risks in a state" (1931, p. 53).

Uncertainty and risk

Cantillon took uncertainty for granted as something inherent in the economic activity of the marketplace. He did not provide a detailed analysis of the nature of risk and uncertainty; he merely related the function of the entrepreneur to uncertainty – and by implication, to risk – and in this way gave economic content to the concept. Since the writings of Frank Knight (1885–1972), it has been customary in economics to distinguish between risk and uncertainty. Knight pointed out that some forms of risk can be mitigated by insurance. To be insurable, there must be a known probability distribution associated with risk, either because of large numbers of individuals exposed to risk or because of repeated exposures to the same risk of the same individual.[1]

Although we cannot credit Cantillon with this distinction, it is reasonably clear that the concept of uncertainty that is central to his analysis is not of the insurable kind. In Cantillon's world, not only is the information about the future unknown, it is also for the most part unknowable. While insurance companies tend to underwrite losses from named perils that are calculated to occur with predictable frequency, they do not typically insure against errors in judgment. Yet Cantillon's entrepreneurs are constantly called upon to exercise their business judgment, and if they guess wrong, they must pay the price.

An astute businessman, Cantillon was obviously aware of institutional arrangements that could be invoked to limit risk. But these things were of little consequence to his theory of entrepreneurship. His discussion of uncertainty is cast in the sense of things unknowable. This kind of uncertainty, which we now call "Knightian uncertainty," is inherent in the nature of competitive (rivalrous) market activity, so there is literally no way to separate the concepts of competition and entrepreneurship in Cantillon's vision of the economy. One is a consequence of the other.

Capital and entrepreneurship

One of the perpetual points of contention in competing theories of entrepreneurship is to what extent the roles of entrepreneur and capitalist can be separated. In any business enterprise, capital is usually placed at risk. If the entrepreneur does not also supply capital, in what sense can he be said to bear risk? Does a risk-bearing theory of entrepreneurship require that an entrepreneur own certain capital assets that are staked in the game of profit and loss? If the capitalist and the entrepreneur are one and the same, then it becomes difficult, if not impossible, to identify the return to each function. But if they are not the same, in what sense does the entrepreneur bear risk? Can there be any such thing as a loss if one has nothing to lose?

Cantillon was more expansive on this issue than many of his successors. It is clear that his entrepreneur must risk something, but it need not be capital in the pecuniary sense. He seemed to appreciate the modern concept of human capital, even though he did not actually formulate the notion. Cantillon referred to "entrepreneurs of their own labor who need no capital to establish themselves," using examples from commerce (chimney sweeps, water carriers), art (painters), and science (physicians, lawyers). He even included beggars and robbers as entrepreneurs (Cantillon 1931, p. 53).

Contemporary economics recognizes that even the penniless entrepreneur incurs potential losses to the extent that he faces opportunity costs for his time and talents. Consider an individual with no means of his own. Suppose he foresees an opportunity that promises an uncertain rate of return, and he borrows capital at a fixed, contractual rate of interest. If the enterprise does so badly that the borrower cannot repay the contracted amount of principle and interest, the financial loss falls solely on the lender. But as S. M. Kanbur (1980, p. 493) argues, the gains and losses of any enterprise must be evaluated relative to the opportunity cost of the enterprise. If a prospective entrepreneur has open to him a safe return in an alternative occupation, his decision to be entrepreneurial involves the possibility of loss – he could end up worse off than if he had taken up a safe occupation. This is the sense in which the prospective entrepreneur faces risks.

For the man of means who foresees and acts on an uncertain opportunity, the problem remains how to separate his risk-bearing role as capitalist from his risk-bearing role as entrepreneur. Conceptually, it is possible to do this, but we must look to the *colleganza* of thirteenth-century Venice or the *societas maris* of ancient Greece for a working model. In these arrangements the functions of capitalist and entrepreneur were separate; the former was an investing partner and the latter a traveling/managing partner. It should be expected that the opportunity cost of the capital in such an arrangement will be different from the opportunity cost of the entrepreneurial effort, and it is in proportion to these different costs that the respective risks have to be conceptualized and, ultimately, measured.

A harbinger of the future

Cantillon argued that the origin of entrepreneurship lies in the lack of perfect foresight individuals have about the future. Rather than consider this lack of foresight a defect of the market system, Cantillon accepted it as part of the human condition. Uncertainty is a pervasive fact of everyday life, and those who must deal with it continually in their economic decisions are entrepreneurs. Consequently it is the function of the entrepreneur, not his personality, that counts for economic analysis. Cantillon was quite emphatic that this function lies at the very heart of a market system, and that without it, the market as we know it does not operate.

Some other aspects of Cantillon's conception are noteworthy. His portrayal of the entrepreneur's role in a market economy has a distinct supply-side emphasis. His entrepreneur does not create demand through new production or merchandising techniques; he merely follows the dictates of a class of fashion leaders (the landlords). The entrepreneur thus provides appropriate goods or services at the right time and place in order to satisfy preordained consumer wants. To be effective, he must be forward-looking. He must be alert, for when particular supplies and demands do not match, the theory calls for the entrepreneur to spring into action. But Cantillon's entrepreneur is not required to be innovative in the strict sense of the term.

The kind of action that engages the entrepreneur's effort is not limited to production, moreover. This is clear from the above passages about middlemen and retailers, as well as from Cantillon's recognition of the arbitrageur as an entrepreneur. Noting the opportunities for profit created by price differences between the countryside and Paris, Cantillon (1931, pp. 150–2) asserted that as long as they can cover transportation costs, entrepreneurs "will buy at a low price the products of the villages and will transport them to the Capital [city] to be sold there at a higher price."

Even a pure arbitrage action such as this involves some uncertainty on the entrepreneur's part. The arbitrageur can perceive that a product sells for one price at one place and at a higher price somewhere else; but if he buys in the first to sell in the second, he must be careful. The transactions are not instantaneous, and something might occur in the interim to change seemingly certain profits into losses.

Although we cannot attribute to Cantillon – nor to any early economist – a complete theory of profit, it is noteworthy that he recognized the legitimacy (and necessity) of entrepreneurial profits in order that the function of the entrepreneur be carried out. Thus he established the economic and social necessity of profit early in the history of economic theory.

We believe that Cantillon's conception of the entrepreneur is extremely important to a proper understanding of the concept in economic analysis. But his view did not predominate, nor was it complete in itself. It was myopic in at least one important respect. Cantillon excluded the "Prince," the landlords, and certain laborers from uncertainty. Today we recognize that economic uncertainty is more pervasive than he allowed. Ludwig von Mises (1949, p. 253) was correct when he asserted that "No proprietor of any means of production, whether they are represented in tangible goods or in money, remains untouched by the uncertainty of the future." Cantillon's notion of entrepreneurship needed to be widened, and at a much later date it was, by Knight and by von Mises. But that is another story.

Cantillon began an important analytical tradition in eighteenth-century France. Based on the idea of a circular flow of aggregate income, he propounded a vision of how a capitalist economy works, giving the entrepreneur a pivotal role. As a result, continental economists remained much more alert to the significance of the entrepreneur than did their British counterparts (at least from Adam Smith to John Stuart Mill). The full flowering of the concept, however, was neither rapid nor direct.

After Cantillon's death, economic analysis in France was dominated by a group of writers who called themselves simply "the Economists." As the term economist became more generic, however, historians began to refer to this particular group of French writers as "the Physiocrats" (the term 'physiocracy' means rule of nature). It was a singular group with a singular leader, François Quesnay (1694–1774). Quesnay shared Cantillon's basic economic vision, and he elaborated Cantillon's notion of the circular flow of wealth by developing an explicit analytical model, which he called the *Tableau Économique*. It was the first mathematical formulation of a general equilibrium system.

François Quesnay

Quesnay entered economics in his sixties, after enjoying considerable success as a physician and author of books on medicine, biology, and philosophy. His renown as a physician brought him into the court of Louis XV, where he personally attended Madame de Pompadour. In economics his fame rests on his pioneer contributions to national income analysis and his acknowledged leadership of the first cohesive school of economic thought. Quesnay's ability to attract adherents to his views stemmed in part from his magnetic personality and in part from the substance of his analysis. That analysis was rich in theoretic and policy implications, but its full import is not at issue here. We are more interested in the contributions of physiocracy to the theory of entrepreneurship.

Quesnay and his band of disciples analyzed the nature and operation of agrarian capitalism. Their analytic system features three economic classes, which can be distinguished from each other by their respective economic functions. A proprietary class owns property rights in the land that it leases to the productive class (i.e., farmers), who in turn produce the raw materials demanded by a third class, the artisans. The unique feature of physiocracy is that it attributes the production of an economic surplus to agriculture and agriculture alone. This surplus is measured by the value of agricultural output over its costs, and it is claimed by the proprietors in the form of rent that is annually paid to the owners of land.

A chief merit of Quesnay's analysis is that it underscores the vital importance of capital to economic growth. In the physiocratic system, capital comes from the landlords, who are best positioned to accumulate wealth. Entrepreneurs are present in the economy as farmers. Quesnay (1888, pp. 218–19) distinguished between small-scale farming (*petite culture*) and large-scale farming (*grande culture*), depicting the entrepreneur as the operator of a large farm. He described the rich farmer as an entrepreneur who "manages and makes his business profitable by his intelligence and his wealth." He had in mind a capitalist farmer who owns and manages his business on land owned by another. Thus his entrepreneur is the independent owner of a business.

Quesnay's emphasis on individual energy, intelligence, and wealth is suggestive, but he did not develop the idea of the entrepreneur further, nor did he extend its application beyond agriculture. In general, physiocracy ignored the notion of the entrepreneur as a leader of industry. In fact, its adherents maintained that manufacturing is "sterile" because it is incapable of yielding a surplus.

Abbé Nicolas Baudeau

One writer in particular among Quesnay's disciples developed a theory of entrepreneurship that foreshadowed future developments. He was a clergyman, the Abbé Nicolas Baudeau (1730–92), who began as a foe of physiocracy but later converted to its system. Baudeau treated the agricultural entrepreneur as a risk-bearer, in the manner of Cantillon, but he added a distinctly modern twist. He made the entrepreneur an innovator as well, one who invents and applies new techniques or ideas in order to reduce his costs and thereby raise his profit. These new aspects of entrepreneurship – invention and innovation – represent an important advance over Cantillon's theory because they anticipate the twentieth-century reformulation of entrepreneurship by Schumpeter, whose theory of "creative destruction" dominates contemporary discussions of the subject.

Baudeau's notion of entrepreneurship paralleled Cantillon's but only to a point. Consider the nature of risk faced by the agricultural entrepreneur. The rent he pays to the landlord is the surplus of farm revenue over necessary costs of production, including some payment for his own services. For the tenant farmer, rent is a cost determined in advance of production. The Physiocrats favored stabilizing these costs as much as possible through long-term leases, while wage rates were usually fixed at or near subsistence levels. Thus the farmer operating with a long-term lease faced certain fixed costs but uncertain harvests and hence uncertain sales prices. This is precisely the situation of Cantillon's entrepreneur, as we have seen.

Where Baudeau went beyond Cantillon was in emphasizing and analyzing the significance of ability. Baudeau underscored the importance of "intelligence," the entrepreneur's ability to collect and process knowledge and information. Intelligence – knowledge and the ability to act – also gives the entrepreneur a measure of control, so that he is not a mere pawn to the capitalist. Baudeau's entrepreneur is an active agent who seeks to increase production and reduce costs (Baudeau 1910, p. 46).

Physiocratic writings are replete with proposals to improve agricultural techniques, many of which were oriented toward the upgrading of human capital or the dissemination of better information. Hoselitz (1960, pp. 246–7) listed several of their proposals: translation of English texts on agriculture; nationwide distribution of handbooks and guides describing new tools, crops, or procedures; prizes; honors; agricultural research; model farms; and pilot programs. The Physiocrats were convinced that when the right knowledge became available, profit opportunities would induce desirable innovations. The entrepreneur as innovator thus appeared relatively early in economic literature.

Baudeau's theory of entrepreneurship presupposes that economic events fall into two categories: those that are subject to human control and those that are not. To the extent that the entrepreneur confronts events under his control, his success depends upon knowledge and ability. To the extent that he confronts events beyond his control, he places himself at risk. In this sense, Baudeau's theory of entrepreneurship is more general than Cantillon's, which concentrated on the effects of uncertainty without reference to administrative control.

Anne-Robert-Jacques Turgot

A. R. J. Turgot's (1727–81) place in history is assured by his distinguished administrative career in French government, culminating in his service as finance minister to Louis XVI from 1774 to 1776. Born to a Norman family of ancient nobility, Turgot was a gifted and precocious young man whose interests ranged widely. One of his many gifts was lucid exposition in the field of economics, and, although he resisted the label of economist (Meek 1973), his chief accomplishment as a writer was in mapping out the theory of an entrepreneurial economy.

Turgot's ideas did not coincide at all points with those of physiocracy. He was, however, on good terms with the members of Quesnay's inner circle, and he extended the theory of entrepreneurship by establishing the ownership of capital as a separate economic function in business. Turgot's capitalist must decide whether to loan his capital to someone else or to invest it in a business enterprise of his own. If he chooses the latter, he must further choose land, manufacturing, or commerce as a form of investment. If he purchases land, he becomes both landowner and capitalist. If he invests in various kinds of goods required for his particular business, he becomes an entrepreneur as well as a capitalist. And if he decides to lend his funds in the form of money, he remains a capitalist only. Unlike Cantillon, Turgot did not anticipate the notion of a "pure" entrepreneur.

In Turgot's scheme of things, the ownership of capital is a qualification for becoming an entrepreneur, but the two functions are nevertheless distinct. One can be a capitalist without being an entrepreneur, but one cannot be an entrepreneur without also being a capitalist. The distinguishing feature of Turgot's entrepreneur, therefore, is not his capital but his labor. The entrepreneur looks to his own labor for his distinctive return.

Turgot reasoned that capital can be employed in different channels: agriculture, manufacturing, or commerce. Employed actively in either of these channels, capital should produce more profit than if merely used to purchase land, because the former requires "much care and labor" by an entrepreneur. Capital may also be employed in a manner that does not require "much care and labor" – for example, to purchase an annuity that provides a future stream of income. But this would not constitute an entrepreneurial action in Turgot's scheme of things. Thus Turgot (1977, p. 86) declared:

> It is necessary then, that, besides the interest of his capital, the entrepreneur should draw every year a profit to recompense him for his care, his labor, his talents and his risks, and to furnish him in addition that which he may replace the annual wear and tear of his advances, which he is obliged from the very first to convert into effects which are liable to deterioration and which are, moreover, exposed to all kinds of accidents.

Ronald Meek (1973) has argued that Cantillon analyzed a society in which the capitalist-entrepreneur was just beginning to separate himself from the ranks of independent workmen, whereas Turgot analyzed an economy in which this process had been completed and in which the capitalist system had consolidated itself in all fields of economic activity. In his *Reflections on the Formation and Distribution of Wealth* (1766), Turgot painted a clear picture of an economy in which capitalism embraces all spheres of production. In his view, the "industrious" classes are divided into entrepreneurs and hired workers. He insisted on a sharp, but somewhat artificial, differentiation between the profit of the former and the wage of the latter. He also maintained that free competition is widespread and monopoly nonexistent; that land ownership is merely another kind of investment in capital; and that a general glut of goods is impossible because savings are transformed immediately into investment. He did not incorporate into his theory any built-in specification about technological progress, nor any hint that the entrepreneur is an innovator (or anything more than a capitalist-laborer), nor did he emphasize the dynamic aspects of the economy.

It is instructive to compare Turgot's representation of the entrepreneur with Quesnay's and Baudeau's. Although Quesnay did not elaborate a complete theory of entrepreneurship, his portrayal of the entrepreneur as a farmer who produces value by "his intelligence and his wealth" contains an abundance of hidden meaning that subsequently provided a point of departure for both Baudeau and Turgot. Baudeau added elements of organization, innovation, and risk. Turgot ignored innovation but stressed supervision, and he generalized the entrepreneurial function to all sectors of the economy. Hoselitz (1960) placed Turgot's theory of entrepreneurship midway between the early French view, which holds the entrepreneur to be chiefly a risk-bearer (e.g., Cantillon and to some extent Baudeau) or a coordinator of production (e.g., Say and to some extent Baudeau), and the English view, which saw the entrepreneur chiefly as a capitalist.

Jean-Baptiste Say

Continuing a French tradition inaugurated by Cantillon, J. B. Say (1767–1832) put the entrepreneur at the core of the entire process of production and distribution. Hoselitz (1960) claims that Say's inspiration and strong views on the subject came from his practical experience as an industrial entrepreneur (he managed a textile mill in Pas-de-Calais) rather than from his acquaintance with other French economists. Nevertheless, Say embellished a concept of the entrepreneur that was fundamentally Turgot's – minus the common link to the capitalist.

Say developed his treatment of entrepreneurship most fully in the later editions of his *Traité d'Économie Politique* (*A Treatise on Political Economy*)

(1803) and in his *Cours Complet d'Économie Politique Pratique* (1828–9). His analysis proceeds on two different levels. On the one hand, he employed empirical descriptions of what entrepreneurs in his day actually did under existing institutional constraints. On the other hand, he exposed and analyzed the central function of the entrepreneur independently of any particular social framework. In this last effort Say moved toward a general theory of entrepreneurship.

As we have asserted, the vigor of entrepreneurial activity depends upon the composition, distribution, and security of property rights. Because entrepreneurial activity is profit seeking, it requires incentives to propel it. These incentives are provided by the structure of property rights within a representative government. Say (1845 [1803], p. 127) was quite clear on this, avowing that "political economy recognizes the right of property solely as the most powerful of all encouragements to the multiplication of wealth." Furthermore, where private property exists in reality as well as in right, "then, and then only, can the sources of production, namely land, capital, and industry, attain their utmost degree of fecundity."

Say's theory of the entrepreneur is part of a threefold division of human industry into distinct operations. The first step is the scientific one. Before any product, such as a bicycle, can be made, certain knowledge about the nature and purpose of it must be understood. It must be known, for example, that a wheel is capable of continuous, circular motion and that a force exerted on a chain and sprockets can propel the wheel forward. The second step, the entrepreneurial one, is the application of this knowledge to a useful purpose (i.e., the development of a mechanism with one or more wheels that is capable of transporting someone from one place to another). The final step, the productive one, is the manufacture of the item by manual labor.

Say's entrepreneur performs a social function, even though Say does not make him a member of a distinct social class. He is a principal agent of production whose role is vital to the production of utility. His applications of knowledge must not be mere random events. They must meet a "market" test; that is, in order to be entrepreneurial, each application must lead to the creation of value or utility. This requires sound judgment, one of the key characteristics of Say's entrepreneur. According to Say, an entrepreneur must be able to estimate customers' needs and the means to satisfy them; he may lack the personal knowledge of science, and he can avoid dirtying his own hands by employing others, but he must not lack judgment, for without it he might "produce at great expense something which has no value" (Say 1840 [1828–9], vol. 1, p. 100).

Say's entrepreneur is an economic catalyst – a pivotal figure. But Say did not follow Cantillon's lead in making uncertainty the mainstay of entrepreneurship. Risk is incidental to Say's notion of entrepreneurship because he saw no necessary dependency of entrepreneurial activity upon capital accumulation. For the first time in economic literature, entrepreneurial activity became virtually synonymous with management, in the contemporary sense of that term. Management may, but does not necessarily, supply capital to the enterprise. And Say had no difficulty, theoretically speaking, separating the entrepreneurial function from the capitalist function, even though both functions could be, and often were, combined in the same person.

In the final analysis, Say's entrepreneur is a superintendent and an administrator. This person:

> requires a combination of moral qualities that are not often found together. Judgment, perseverance, and a knowledge of the world, as well as of business. He is called upon to estimate, with tolerable accuracy, the importance of the specific product, the probable amount of the demand, and the means of its production: at one time he must employ a great number of hands; at another, buy or order the raw material, collect laborers, find consumers, and give at all times a rigid attention to order and economy; in a word, he must possess the art of superintendence and administration. (Say 1845 [1803], pp. 330–1)

Hoselitz (1960) drew two distinctions between Say and Cantillon, both of which are questionable. One distinction is that Say's entrepreneur is a universal mediator (e.g., between landlord and capitalist; between scientist and laborers; between producers and consumers), whereas Cantillon's entrepreneur is not. This claim is dubious because Say makes no allowance for the most active of mediators, the arbitrageur, whereas Cantillon explicitly recognizes the arbitrageur as an entrepreneur. Moreover, Cantillon gives the entrepreneur the sole function of mediating discrepancies between quantities demanded and quantities supplied in a market economy. By sheer frequency of reference in the *Essai*, the entrepreneur is virtually everywhere in this capacity.

Hoselitz's second distinction is that, unlike Cantillon and the Physiocrats, Say does not restrict his entrepreneur to a capitalist society. Technically this is correct, but Say's arguments in general were calculated to reaffirm the desirable social consequences of individual self-interest, and he was fully aware (as was Adam Smith) that a market economy provided the social framework that permitted the full flowering of self-interest. On a lesser point, however, Hoselitz is quite correct: Say's entrepreneur (mediator) may appear in a primitive society before capital has been accumulated. In other words, the entrepreneur could direct and supervise raw materials and manual labor without the application of capital. But surely the same holds for Cantillon's beggar and robber "entrepreneurs."

One aspect of Say's theory is particularly important because it established the traditional paradigm and also provided a point of departure for future breaks with tradition. Say's entrepreneur may be characterized as a "guardian" of equilibrium. The "judgment" extolled by Say as a requisite of entrepreneurial activity is confined to relations within a production process and does not extend beyond that process to the discovery of new processes or to changes inspired by a new social structure. Because he did not see a necessary relationship between capital accumulation (investment) and entrepreneurial activity, Say did not place the entrepreneur in a dynamic environment. His role was conceived within a purely stationary equilibrium characterized by the equality of prices of products with their costs of production. The primary source of entrepreneurial income in this system is not profit as a risk premium but rather wages as a payment for a highly skilled type of scarce labor.

In later works, Say (1845 [1803]) did portray the entrepreneur as a kind of superior laborer. He extended the analogy to include a kind of "market" for entrepreneurs, in which their wages were determined by supply and demand, and he went to some length in discussing the determinants of entrepreneurial supply. From a narrow theoretic standpoint, his treatment of the entrepreneur was a step forward because it distinguished between the respective contributions in production of human and non-human agents. But it did not move the concept any closer to a "pure" theory of entrepreneurship.[2] By portraying the entrepreneur chiefly as a superior form of labor, Say consciously or unconsciously directed attention away from the uniqueness of the entrepreneur and thus from his role as a force of change in a dynamic economy.

A. L. C. Destutt de Tracy and Henri Saint-Simon

Say was a dominant influence on nineteenth-century French economics. Like Smith, he was able to capture the spirit of his times, and the organizational schema of his Treatise proved to be much more amenable to the pedagogy of economics, which was becoming commonplace among institutions of higher learning. It therefore became a major "textbook" at universities on both sides of the Atlantic, particularly in America, where it was welcomed by Thomas Jefferson and its adoption was widespread. New entrants in the competition for ideas soon appeared, however. Among the many, two are especially prominent – one for its clarity, the other for its prophecy.

A. L. C. Destutt de Tracy (1754–1836) and Henri Saint-Simon (1760–1825) shared the advantage of noble birth at a time when the rank and privileges of nobility in France were threatened on all sides. Strictly speaking, neither was an economist, although both confronted social issues that could not be extricated from economic considerations. Destutt de Tracy was one of the last *philosophes* and, along with Say, one of the earliest members of the French liberal school. He coined the term "ideology," by which he meant the science of ideas. Only later did the term take on a pejorative sense, primarily because Marx treated it with disdain. There is no subject in economics to which Destutt de Tracy contributed greatly, but he nevertheless had the remarkable ability of attracting great minds. He rejected the physiocratic notion of value, substituting in its place a labor theory that was subsequently endorsed by Ricardo.

Like the Physiocrats, Destutt de Tracy extolled the virtues of an agricultural economy. But he looked beyond the narrow limits of agriculture and grasped the essence of a nascent capitalism that was far more pervasive than mere farming. He was struck first and foremost by the prevalence of economic activities. "The whole of society," he wrote, "is but a continual succession of exchanges;" consequently, "we are all more or less commercial" (Tracy 1817, p. 35). Commerce and society are one and the same thing" (Tracy 1817, p. 68). In this formulation of society, Tracy gave the entrepreneur wide berth. Capital precedes all enterprise, large or small, he asserted, so the enterpriser must have capital to carry out his function. But are the entrepreneur and the capitalist necessarily the same?

Revealing the combined influences of Turgot and Say, Destutt de Tracy answered in the affirmative. The world is divided into theory, application, and execution, he wrote. Science provides theory; the entrepreneur applies science to commerce; and labor produces the end product that science and application creates. Destutt de Tracey (1970 [1817], p. 36, 39–40) asserts that the man of science and the workman:

> will always be in the pay of the entrepreneur, for it is not sufficient to know how to aid an enterprise with the head or the hands: there must be first an enterprise; and he who undertakes it, is necessarily the person who chooses, employs, and pays those who co-operate. Now who is he who can undertake it? It is the man who already has funds, with which he can meet the first expenses of establishment and supplies, and pay wages till the moment of the first returns.

Like Cantillon, Destutt de Tracy underscored the incertitude of the entrepreneur's reward. He recognized risk and opportunity costs as factors affecting the supply of entrepreneurship, but he based the success or failure of the entrepreneur "solely on the quantity of utility he has been able to produce, on the necessity that others are under of procuring it, and ... on the means they have of paying him for it."

Claude Henri de Rouvroy, Comte de Saint-Simon, was a pixilated figure in a period that abounded in colorful characters. He is usually not taken seriously by economists because his doctrine is believed to contain elements of socialism and, ultimately, mysticism. He was a prolific writer and visionary who indiscriminately mixed nonsense with clairvoyant prophecy. Above all else, he was obsessed with the nature of social and economic change. His interest in economics sprang from his zeal to rationalize the social order.

Saint-Simon believed that social policy should be adapted to the needs of production. He welcomed the disintegration of feudalism and the advent of its replacement, industrialism. *Industrialisme* meant the triumph of technology over backwardness, of science and reason over superstition and custom. Saint-Simon's vision of the industrial society is almost a carbon copy of John Kenneth Galbraith's (1967) technocracy. Edward S. Mason (1931) referred to Saint-Simon's goal as "the rationalisation of industry." What this means is the ascendancy of the business leader, the economic "expert" whose skills are tempered in the crucible of competition. Saint-Simon's society of producers requires the sort of person who can apply established principles toward the attainment of recognized goals. Ultimately this demands that business is brought into politics and that politicians become producers.

Whether or not society would remain competitive if reorganized along the lines suggested by Saint-Simon in the eighteenth century or Galbraith in the twentieth century is problematic. Although Saint-Simon gave the entrepreneur a prominent place in his economic structure, he did not develop the concept beyond what is implied in the notion of a business leader. Nor did he concern himself with economic analysis, per se, which of necessity precedes the task of reorganization. He was content with the economic analysis and the economic policy of Smith and Say. And in the end his disciples transformed his doctrine into a kind of religion, thus eroding its appeal to serious economists in search of operational tools of analysis.

Postscript

Even a cursory review of French economic literature in the eighteenth and early nineteenth centuries reveals that the entrepreneur was regarded as a vital component of a market economy. The development of the concept, however, did not follow strict evolutionist principles. These early writers anticipated a number of aspects of the entrepreneur that would resurface in later writings, including the entrepreneur as one who assumes risk; supplies financial capital; is an industrial leader, manager, and coordinator of economic resources; acts as an arbitrageur; and allocates resources. One lonely voice even presaged the entrepreneur as innovator. As economists attempted to discover and elucidate the laws of the market, variations were introduced in the definition and function of the entrepreneur, first by one author then by another – even among writers who shared a common language.

On other shores, writers of different languages and cultures also dealt with the concept. We turn our attention next to developments in England and Germany during the high time of classical economics, *c.* 1776 to 1870.

3   The English school of thought

English custom before Adam Smith

There were three commonly used English equivalents of the French term "entrepreneur" in the eighteenth century: "adventurer," "projector," and "undertaker." The first term was applied in the fifteenth century to merchants operating at some risk and in the seventeenth century to land speculators, farmers, and those who directed certain public-works projects. During the eighteenth century, the term adventurer gradually gave way to the more general term undertaker, which had become synonymous with an ordinary businessman by the time Adam Smith emerged as a progenitor of political economy. The term projector was equivalent to the other two in a fundamental sense, but it more often had the pejorative connotation of a cheat and a rogue. The word undertaker was not only used more often, it also took on more varied meanings, and its history more or less paralleled the development of its French counterpart.

At first the term undertaker simply referred to someone who set out to do a job or complete a project, but the concept evolved into that of government contractor – someone who, at his own financial risk, performed a task imposed on him by government. The term was later extended to include those individuals who held exclusive franchises from the Crown or the parliament, such as tax farmers or persons commissioned to drain the fens. By and by the government connection was dropped, and the term simply came to designate someone involved in a risky project from which an uncertain profit might be derived (Hoselitz 1960, pp. 240–2).[1] For unknown reasons, by the nineteenth century the word undertaker had acquired the special meaning of an arranger of funerals. Partly because of the way in which Adam Smith employed the term, undertaker was eventually replaced by the term "capitalist" among English writers.

Prodigals, projectors, and Adam Smith's prudent man

The *locus classicus* of economic analysis in the eighteenth century was Adam Smith's *An Inquiry into the Nature and Causes of the Wealth of Nations* (1776). But Smith discussed entrepreneur types earlier, in *The Theory of Moral Sentiments* (1759). In *Wealth of Nations*, the entrepreneur is encountered in three different forms: the adventurer, the projector, and the undertaker. Smith speaks disparagingly of the first two and with unqualified approbation only of the undertaker, who he identified with "the prudent man" – a concept developed at length in *Moral Sentiments*.

According to Smith, adventurers are those who hazard their capital on the most difficult of enterprises, spurred on by unbounded confidence in their success despite extraordinary risks. Smith (1976b [1776], vol. 1, p. 128) attributed a measure of irrationality to this kind of behavior, because although "the ordinary rate of profit always rises more or less with the risk, it does not … seem to rise in proportion to it, or so as to compensate it completely." Adventurers, therefore, are not stable agents in a theory of economic development; although a "bold adventurer may sometimes acquire a considerable fortune by two or three successful speculations;" he "is just as likely to lose one by two or three unsuccessful ones" (Smith 1976b [1776], vol. 1, pp. 130–1).

According to *Postlethwayt's Dictionary*, an established authority in Smith's day, projectors are of two types. One type is cunning, lawless, scheming, and cheating; the other possesses ingenuity and integrity and engages in honest invention. Postlethwayt added that because "there were always more geese than swans, the number of the latter are very inconsiderable, in comparison with the former." Owing, perhaps, to the inconsiderable number of honest projectors, Smith (1976b [1776], vol. 2, p. 562) was critical of the first class of projectors, who devise "expensive and uncertain projects … which bring bankruptcy upon the greater part of the people who engage in them," such as the "search after new silver and gold mines." In this way projectors are injurious to society because "every injudicious and unsuccessful project in agriculture, mines, fisheries, trade, or manufactures, tends … to diminish the funds destined for the maintenance of productive labor" (Smith 1976b [1776], vol. 1, p. 341). Identifying projectors with prodigals, Smith (1976b [1776], vol. 1, p. 340) minced few words in his judgment: "Every prodigal appears to be a public enemy, and every frugal man a public benefactor."

Following Postlethwayt, however, Smith allowed that not all projectors are prodigals. Of the prudent man, Smith (1976a [1759], vol. 1, p. 215) said that:

[I]f he enters into any new projects or enterprises, they are likely to be well concerted and well prepared. He can never be hurried or drove into them by any necessity, but has always time and leisure to deliberate soberly and coolly concerning what are likely to be their consequences.

The prudent man is frugal (i.e., he accumulates capital) and is an agent of slow but steady progress.

This kind of treatment in which the entrepreneur is either a menace or a boon leaves the concept of entrepreneurship muddled. As a result, erudite scholars have derided Smith. Joseph Spengler (1959, pp. 8–9) characterized Smith's entrepreneur as essentially passive: "a prudent, cautious, not overly imaginative fellow, who adjusts to circumstances rather than brings about their modification." Joseph Schumpeter, who established his own distinctly dynamic notion of entrepreneurship, was unsympathetic to Smith in many ways, not least of which was his view of the role of the entrepreneur. According to Schumpeter (1954, p. 555), if pressed, Smith would not have denied that no business runs by itself, yet:

> this is exactly the over-all impression his readers get. The merchant or master accumulates 'capital' – this is really his essential function – and with this 'capital' he hires 'industrious people', that is, workmen, who do the rest. In doing so he exposes these means of production to risk of loss; but beyond this, all he does is to supervise his concern in order to make sure that the profits find their way to his pocket.

Enzo Pesciarelli (1989, p. 525) has defended Smith, claiming that his discussion of that class of society "who live by profit" emphasizes the planning element as well as the possession of capital. Pesciarelli draws textual support from the following passage in *Wealth of Nations*:

> The plans and projects of the employers of stock regulate and direct all the most important operations of labour, and profit is the end proposed by all those plans and projects. Merchants and master manufacturers are, in this order, the two classes of people who commonly employ the largest capitals. … As during their whole lives they are engaged in plans and projects, they have frequently more acuteness of understanding than the greater part of country gentlemen.
>
> (Smith 1976b [1776], vol. 1, p. 266)

Pesciarelli makes a number of useful points, but even so, he tacitly admits that Smith's works have to be mined carefully to find the few useful gems that make up his contribution to the subject. Collecting the various hints sprinkled throughout *Wealth of Nations* and supplementing them with Smith's "prudent man" concept developed in *The Theory of Moral Sentiments*, Pesciarelli (1989, pp. 527–8) offers the following composite picture of Smith's entrepreneur.

- Smith's undertaker faces risk and uncertainty.
- Smith's undertaker formulates plans and projects in an effort to earn profit.
- Smith's undertaker seeks out the necessary capital for implementation of his planned undertaking.
- Smith's undertaker combines and organizes the productive factors.
- Smith's undertaker inspects and directs production.

If one accepts Pesciarelli's reconstructed view, it would seem to put Smith rather loosely in the tradition of Cantillon, a writer known to Smith by the time he wrote *Wealth of Nations*.

The idea that profit is determined by the labor of organization and direction comes from Turgot. Smith rejected this notion, arguing that labor is labor, regardless of who expends it.

> The profits of stock bear no proportion to the quantity, the hardship, or the ingenuity of this supposed labour of inspection and direction. They are regulated altogether by the value of the stock employed, and are greater or smaller in proportion to the extent of this stock.
>
> (Smith 1976b [1776], vol. 1, p. 66)

Yet in correcting Turgot's error, Smith appears to confound production goods, capital, profits and interest, which led to the charges of ambivalence (or neglect) that we have seen.

Charles Tuttle (1927, pp. 507–8) claimed that prevailing business practices of the era account for Smith's failure to differentiate the function of the capitalist from that of the entrepreneur. In England and France at this time, the ownership of capital was prerequisite to becoming the independent head of a business. This fact is reflected in the writings of both Turgot and Smith, each of whom took the ownership of capital for granted; yet Smith gave much stronger emphasis to the ownership of capital as the basis for entrepreneurship.

Missing from Pesciarelli's list of elemental characteristics is any explicit connection between entrepreneur and innovation. We know that Smith was very sensitive to the effects of innovation in a capitalist society. In fact, he was one of the first economic writers to recognize innovation as a professional activity. In a remark on inventions made by workmen, Smith (1976b [1776], vol. 1, p. 21) noted that many improvements in manufacturing are made by workmen, but that a more learned class of men – "who are called philosophers or men of speculation" – also play a key role. Those who belong to this learned class, "whose trade it is not to do anything, but to observe everything … upon that account, are often capable of combining together the powers of the most distant and dissimilar objects." Thomas Edison might easily fit into this group of "philosopher-inventors." This was a potentially fruitful line of inquiry, which, unfortunately, Smith did not develop to any measurable extent.

The eighteenth-century inventor (i.e., Smith's "philosopher" or "speculator") was an amateur by contemporary standards; yet Smith's view of innovation as professional activity was ahead of its time. He held that innovation is the product of the division of labor, which in turn depends on the extent of the market. Innovation therefore appears first in markets that are enlarged by cheap transportation. Opulence and progress thereafter accompany the division of labor, and with this progress the innovator or inventor becomes more specialized, and "the quantity of science is considerably increased."

Jeremy Bentham: The entrepreneur as contractor

Smith's advocacy of usury laws to prevent excessive financial resources from reaching prodigals and projectors struck a discordant note with Jeremy Bentham (1748–1832), a follower of Smith and also an admirer of the French philosophers. Bentham considered it odd (as did many later economists) that the apostle of laissez faire would advocate government intervention in financial markets, which he did by defending a statutory interest rate. Smith's reference to "sober people" in the following passage is an offhand reference to the prudent undertaker, whose actions he approved.

> The legal rate [of interest], it is to be observed, though it ought to be somewhat above, ought not to be much above, the lowest market rate. If the legal rate of interest in Great Britain, for example, was fixed so high as eight or ten per cent the greater part of the money which was to be lent, would be lent to prodigals and projectors, who alone would be willing to give this high interest. Sober people, who will give for the use of money no more than a part of what they are likely to make by the use of it, would not venture into the competition. A great part of the capital of the country would thus be kept out of the hands which were most likely to make a profitable and advantageous use of it, and thrown into those which were most likely to waste and destroy it. Where the legal interest, on the contrary, is fixed but a very little above the lowest market rate, sober people are universally preferred as borrowers, to

prodigals and projectors. The person who lends money, gets nearly as much interest from the former, as he dares to take from the latter, and his money is much safer in the hands of the one set of people than in those of the other. A great part of the capital of the country is thus thrown into the hands in which it is most likely to be employed with advantage.

(Smith 1976b [1776], vol. 1, p. 357)

In his *Defence of Usury* (1787) Bentham detailed how laws against usury limit the overall quantity of capital lent and borrowed and how such laws keep foreign money away from domestic capital markets. Both these effects tend to throttle the activities of successful entrepreneurs and impede economic development. He argued that interest-rate ceilings tend to discriminate against entrepreneurs of new projects; by their sheer novelty, such projects are more risky than those already proven profitable by experience. Moreover, legal restrictions such as usury laws are powerless to pick out bad projects from good ones.

Bentham criticized Smith for underestimating the role of talented individuals whose imagination and inventiveness have been responsible for the progress of nations. He regarded innovation as the driving force behind the development of mankind, and he regarded the projector as the innovator. Hence he reprimanded Smith for lumping prodigals and projectors together. The distinguishing feature of the latter is that they depart from routine patterns of behavior, break away from the common herd, and in the process discover new markets, find new sources of supply, improve existing products, or lower costs of production. To be a projector, Bentham (1952, p. 177) asserted, requires courage and genius, those qualities to which we attribute "all those successive enterprizes by which arts and manufactures have been brought from their original nothing to their present splendor." Projectors create utility, Bentham (1952, p. 170) argued, by affecting improvements, whether such improvements:

consist in the production of any new article adapted to man's use, or in the meliorating the quality, or diminishing the expence, of any of those which are already known to us. It falls, in short, upon every application of the human powers, in which ingenuity stands in need of wealth for its assistant.

The affinity of this view to Schumpeter's is unmistakable.[2]

Pesciarelli argues, cogently, that the nub of controversy between Smith and Bentham is that each had a different view of human progress. And as a by-product of their contrasting views, each had a different conception of the entrepreneur. Bentham's entrepreneur is an exceptional individual, one above the common herd, a minority in society. Smith's entrepreneur is a common type, widespread in society; he is one who exercises self-control in the exercise of economic activity in order to receive the approbation of his fellow man.

> The prudent man unconsciously promotes the interest of society because he consciously sets limits on the pursuit of his own interests. He is the visible promoter of the invisible hand; he is the fulcrum but also the limit of Smith's belief in the working of a self-adjusting mechanism.
>
> (Pesciarelli 1989, pp. 534–5)

These contrasting views lead to different conceptions of economic development. For Bentham economic development is activated by discontinuous changes involving improvements (in the broadest sense) and resulting in a nonlinear path of progress. Smith's notion of economic progress is slow, gradual, uniform, and not subject to sudden variations.

In supporting the cause of the projectors, Bentham, the inventor of the panopticon, was to some extent pleading his own case. The panopticon was the name Bentham gave to his model prison, which involved innovations of both an architectural and an institutional nature. Bentham's ideal prison was circular. All the cells were arranged concentrically around a central pavilion, which contained an inspector, or at most a small number of inspectors. From his central outpost the inspector could easily see everything that was going on, yet he was rendered invisible by a system of blinds. This arrangement also allowed prison administrators, even outside visitors, to inspect the prisoners without being seen. According to Bentham, this constant scrutiny of the prisoners would deprive them of the power, and even the will, to do evil. Bentham was never able to attract enough backers to make his model prison a reality, and the London site that he proposed for his model prison was subsequently occupied by the Tate Gallery.

Bentham's brother, Samuel, devised the architectural idea behind the panopticon, which he first applied in Russia. Bentham's unique contribution was an administrative innovation that is more to the point of our subject than is the general problem of prison reform. Bentham completed the architectural innovation of the Panopticon by introducing an administrative arrangement that involved management by contract. What is especially interesting about this arrangement is that its success depends on the dynamic activities of the entrepreneur and the proper structuring of economic incentives.

To Bentham, true reform would occur in prisons only if the administrative plan simultaneously protected convicts against the harshness of their warders and protected society against the wastefulness of administrators. The choice, as he saw it, was between contract management and trust management.

Élie Halévy (1955, p. 84) explained the differences between these two administrative arrangements:

> Contract-management is management by a man who treats with the government, and takes charge of the convicts at so much a head and applies their time and industry to his personal profit, as does a master with his apprentices. Trust-management is management by a single individual or by a committee, who keep up the establishment at the public expense, and pay into the treasury the products of the convicts' work.

In Bentham's mind, trust management could not establish the proper junction of interest and duty on the part of the entrepreneur. Its success therefore depends on "public interest" as a motivating factor. Like his proclaimed mentor, Smith, Bentham had much more confidence in individual self-interest as the spur to human action. The beauty of contract management was that it brought about an artificial identity of interests between the public on the one hand and the entrepreneur on the other. The entrepreneur in Bentham's scheme was an independent contractor who "purchased," through competitive bid, the right to run the prison, thereby also acquiring title to whatever profits might be earned by the application of convict labor. Such an entrepreneur-manager could maximize his long-term gains by preserving the health and productivity of his worker-convicts. In this manner public interest became entwined with private interest.

In 1787 Bentham completed the idea of contract management by a new administrative arrangement; he thought that life insurance offered an excellent means of joining the interest of one man to the preservation of a number of men. He therefore proposed that, after consulting the appropriate mortality tables, the entrepreneur (prison manager) should be given a fixed sum of money for each convict due to die that year in prison, on the condition that at the end of the year he must pay back the same sum for each convict who had actually died in prison. The difference would be profit for the entrepreneur, who would thereby have an economic incentive to lower the average mortality rate in his prison (Bentham 1962 [1838–43], vol. 4, p. 53).

Aside from the fact that Bentham was virtually alone among British classical economists in his repeated emphasis on the entrepreneur as an agent of economic progress, it is noteworthy that his administrative arrangement of contract management recast the entrepreneur in the position of government contractor, that is, a franchisee who undertakes financial risk in order to obtain an uncertain profit. Bentham also explicitly tied his notion of entrepreneur-contractor to the act of invention. He defended contract management as the proper form of prison administration on the ground that it is a progressive innovation and should therefore be rewarded accordingly, no less than an inventor is rewarded for his successful invention (Bentham 1962 [1838–43], vol. 4, p. 47).

David Ricardo and the "unfortunate legacy"

Bentham and David Ricardo (1772–1823) had different notions about what political economy should be. Ricardo saw political economy as a means to discover general laws of society. Whatever its practical consequences might ultimately be, Ricardo considered economic theory detached from practice. He treated political economy as a science of laws – laws of equilibrium and laws of progress. By contrast, Bentham, like Smith, referred to economics as both art and science, and he paid as much attention to the former as he did to the latter. Bentham and Smith regarded political economy as a branch of politics and legislation, never removed from practice.

We cannot be sure whether it was Bentham's large concern for practice as well as theory that induced him to see the importance of the entrepreneur in economic activity, but in any event, his idea of entrepreneurship did not predominate. Instead, Smith carried the day among economists, and as a result his obscurantism regarding the separation of functions between entrepreneur and capitalist continued to plague classical economics. Fritz Redlich (1966, p. 715) called it an "unfortunate legacy," because to deny the separation of functions between entrepreneur and capitalist implies that profit is not legitimate in a capitalist economy. This legacy was bequeathed to David Ricardo and through him passed on to Karl Marx, who embellished and continued the idea of the capitalist bogey, that is, the parasitic "extortionist" who sucks profit from the "industrious" people of the economy.

Classical economists in general had very little to say about the origin and nature of investment opportunities. This is especially true of Ricardo, who assumed that capitalists act rationally in seeking to maximize profits but ignored the trouble and risk involved in investing. Although he did not fall into the trap of assuming that all investment was profitable, like most classical economists Ricardo treated innovation as mainly external to the economic system. On occasion he supposed that as wealth increased, eventually all further opportunities for profitable investment would disappear. This stands in marked contrast to the Schumpeterian view, which enlarged the scope and breadth of entrepreneurial activity and made it a centerpiece of its theory of economic development.

There is a sense in which Ricardo is more culpable than Smith for his neglect of the entrepreneur. Smith was acquainted with Quesnay, and he may also have known Turgot's work directly. But aside from a difference in emphasis, Smith did not view the entrepreneur/undertaker in terms much different from those of his French counterparts. Ricardo, on the other hand, failed entirely to pursue the suggestion of his contemporary Jean-Baptiste Say, that the entrepreneur is distinguishable from the other agents of production. Smith could not have done so, because his work preceded Say's by almost three decades, but Say had formalized the term "entrepreneur" and given it definition some fourteen years before Ricardo's *On the Principles of Political Economy and Taxation* (1817) appeared. Moreover, at least one version of Say's work was available to Ricardo in English during this fourteen-year period. Yet, as Arthur Cole (1946, p. 3) noted, "Not merely is the term [entrepreneur] itself absent in Ricardo's writings, but no concept of business leaders as agents of change (other than as shadowy bearers of technological improvements) is embraced in his treatment of economic principles." It is noteworthy that in the correspondence between Say and Ricardo, neither the nature nor the role of the entrepreneur is once mentioned, their usual discussion focusing instead on the topic of value.

The decline of British classical economics

More than any other writer after Smith, Ricardo set forth the "research program" that was to occupy the next generation of economists. Consequently, his failure to recognize the entrepreneur as a separate agent of production was a harbinger of later developments in classical economic theory. One exception to this pattern of neglect can be found in the work of John Stuart Mill (1806–73), who cut his teeth on Ricardian economics but also came under the direct (and indirect) influence of Jeremy Bentham. In his youth, Mill served as Bentham's secretary. His family at one time lived on Bentham's London estate, and his father was an ardent disciple of Bentham who took it upon himself to "home-school" his son as evidence of his belief in Benthamite principles.

Mill's *Principles of Political Economy* (1848) is a watershed in British classical economics. It consists of a mature statement of the economic paradigm first enunciated by Smith and successively refined and developed by David Ricardo, Robert Malthus, Nassau Senior, and others. It is also a kind of bridge between the economics of the old school (1776–1870) and the new school (1871–1920). Yet Mill contributed little that was new to the theory of entrepreneurship. He lamented the fact that "undertaker" did not adequately convey the desired economic meaning, and he noted the superiority of the French term for this purpose (Mill 1965 [1848], p. 406n). But throughout his *Principles*, Mill spoke somewhat ambiguously of the entrepreneur and of his economic reward. He identified the functions of the entrepreneur as direction, control, and superintendence. In one place he observed that the qualities of direction and superintendence are always in short supply (Mill 1965 [1848], p. 108), and in another he suggested that superior business talents such as these always receive a kind of rent alongside ordinary profits (Mill 1965 [1848], p. 476), thus approaching von Mangoldt's important innovation on the theory (discussed in Chapter 4). In the final analysis, Mill offered no clear-cut distinction between the capitalist and the entrepreneur, insisting that the return to the latter is composed of a risk premium and a wage of superintendence. This view was representative of most treatments by British classical economists.

Schumpeter (1954, p. 555) claims that Say was the first to assign the entrepreneur a distinct position in the economic process apart from the capitalist, but even Say did not make full use of his own insight, nor did he see clearly all of its analytic possibilities. Bentham was the first Englishman to offer provocative insights into the nature of entrepreneurship beyond Say, but he was more concerned with institutional reform (e.g., the panopticon and other schemes) than with the development of a core of analytic principles that were strictly economic. Mill had read Bentham and Say, but he did not follow the suggestions on entrepreneurship advanced by either writer. He kept the entrepreneur in the background of his distribution theory by focusing mainly on land, labor, and capital as agents of production. By implication, this suggests that the entrepreneur is either a special laborer or a combination of laborer and capitalist. Mill did not seriously entertain the idea of the entrepreneur as innovator. Where he discussed the labor of invention and discovery, for example, Mill treated its reward as merely a kind of wage.

Mill outlined the capitalist's return as the sum of an opportunity cost for postponing consumption (i.e., Nassau Senior's concept of "abstinence"), plus an indemnity for risk of capital, plus the "wages of superintendence." He asserted further that the wages of superintendence are not regulated by the same principle as wages in general. Specifically, he maintained that the wages of superintendence are not advanced from capital, like the wages of other workers, but arise in profit, which is not realized until production is completed.

In Mill's time, the wages of labor were explained by the wages-fund doctrine, which viewed the source of wages as capital (i.e., accumulation) that is advanced to workers prior to realization of final output. In this view, the total amount that can be paid to labor is limited by the amount of capital previously accumulated. Mill's distinction between ordinary wages and the wages of superintendence therefore implies that there is no such limit on the wages of superintendence. But we are still left with the somewhat unhappy alliance of the entrepreneur and the capitalist. Because of this functional "merger," British classical economics offered no focal point for viewing the pivotal role of the entrepreneur in the economic process.

Postscript

The English school of thought is, perhaps, best known for reinforcing the concept of the entrepreneur as one who supplies financial capital. The idea of the entrepreneur as innovator was advanced by Jeremy Bentham, but Bentham's idea did not take root among other classical economists. The Smith–Ricardo–Mill tradition that dominated English classical economic thought essentially preserved a somewhat sterile notion of entrepreneurship.

4   The German tradition

Eighteenth-century German economic thought was associated most closely with cameralism, the study of national finance. Cameralism represented an economic theory in which public revenue was the sole measure of economic prosperity. Not surprisingly, there was little room for the individual entrepreneur in such a field. Owing to the burgeoning influence of Adam Smith and Jean-Baptiste Say, political economy began to gradually displace German cameral science around 1800. By 1814 Say's *Treatise* had been translated into German and was beginning to make an impact on German economics.

Given this belated start to German political economy, it is surprising that the attempt to establish the entrepreneur's profit as a distinctive functional share in the theory of income distribution accelerated faster in Germany than in either France or England. Major advances were made by J. H. von Thünen (1785–1850) and H. K. von Mangoldt (1824–68), with earlier help from Gottlieb Hufeland (1760–1817), Friedrich Hermann (1795–1868), and especially Adolph Riedel (1809–72).

Hufeland (1815) recognized that every wage contains a premium for scarcity. He generalized this idea to explain entrepreneurial profit as a special kind of wage consisting of the "rent of ability". Hermann's (1832) theoretical economics undermined the British classical wages-fund theory by asserting that all factor returns are ultimately paid from consumers' income. Like Hufeland, he generalized the concept of rent to all factors, including the entrepreneur. And like Say, he viewed the entrepreneur as one who organizes production within the institutional structure of a firm.

Riedel (1838) extended Cantillon's conception of the entrepreneur as the economic agent who takes on uncertainty so that others may escape the same uncertainty (e.g., through the establishment of fixed-price contracts). He perceived that uncertainty is inevitable in the acquisition of income and that the entrepreneur provides a useful service to income earners who are risk-averse and who would therefore willingly trade uncertainty for the security of a "sure thing." As a supplier of "certainty," the entrepreneur is rewarded for his foresight or penalized for lack of it. If he sells goods at a price above his contracted fixed-input costs, he gains; if not, he loses. Riedel also explored the notion of the entrepreneur as innovator and as organizer of "team production." By connecting the problems of the organization of firms with the entrepreneurial function of reducing income uncertainty for certain inputs, he anticipated (along with von Mangoldt) the nature of transaction costs later expounded by Ronald Coase (see Chapter 9).

J. H von Thünen

Von Thünen is best known in the history of economics for his contributions to location theory, but in the second volume of *The Isolated State* (1850) he put forth an explanation of profit that clearly distinguished the return of the entrepreneur from that of the capitalist. What von Thünen labeled "entrepreneurial gain" is profit minus (1) interest on invested capital, (2) insurance against business losses, and (3) the wages of management. This residual represents a return to entrepreneurial risk, which von Thünen (1960 [1850], p. 246) identified as *uninsurable risk*, insofar as "there exists no insurance company that will cover all and every risk connected with a business. A part of the risk must always be accepted by the entrepreneur."

As Kanbur (1980) has argued, opportunity costs provide the basis for measuring this element of risk that is uninsurable. Von Thünen (1960 [1850], p. 247) seems to have been alert to this fact, as demonstrated in the following passage:

> He who has enough means to pay to get some knowledge and education for public service has a choice to become either a civil servant or, if equally suited for both kinds of jobs, to become an industrial entrepreneur. If he takes the first job, he is guaranteed subsistence for life; if he chooses the latter, an unfortunate economic situation may take all his property, and then his fate becomes that of a worker for daily wages. Under such unequal expectations for the future what could motivate him to become an entrepreneur if the probability of gain were not much greater than that of loss?

Moreover, von Thünen clearly appreciated the difference between management and entrepreneurship. He maintained that the effort of an entrepreneur working on his own account was different from that of a paid substitute (i.e., "manager"), even if they have the same knowledge and ability. The entrepreneur is forced to bear the anxiety and agitation that accompanies his business gamble. He spends many sleepless nights preoccupied with the single thought of how to avoid catastrophe; whereas the paid substitute can sleep soundly at night, secure in the knowledge of having performed his (minimal) duty. Anyone who has nursed along a new enterprise knows the anxiety that accompanies such entrepreneurial effort.

What is especially interesting about von Thünen's treatment is how he turns the discussion from the trials of the entrepreneur into a kind of "crucible" theory of the development of entrepreneurial talent. The sleepless nights of the entrepreneur are not unproductive; it is then that the entrepreneur makes his plans and arrives at solutions for avoiding business failure. Adversity in the business world thereby becomes a training ground for the entrepreneur. "Necessity is the mother of invention," von Thünen (1960 [1850], p. 248) wrote, "so the entrepreneur through his troubles will become an inventor and explorer in his field." As such, the entrepreneur supplies "greater mental effort in comparison with the paid manager," for which he deserves "compensation for his industry, diligence, and ingenuity." This extra reward is a justifiable payment to the entrepreneur no less than that surplus which is payable to the inventor of a new and useful machine.

What makes this a significant step forward in the theory of entrepreneurship is the fact that von Thünen successfully married the separate strands of entrepreneurial theory that on the one hand characterized the entrepreneur as risk bearer (Cantillon, Mill) and on the other hand portrayed him as innovator (Baudeau, Bentham). Economic analysis having come this far by 1850, we may well question whether Schumpeter took a step backward in the next century by excluding risk-bearing from the nature of entrepreneurship, confining its meaning instead solely to innovative activity (see Chapter 7).

Von Thünen was quite explicit about the fact that there are two elements in entrepreneurial income: a return to entrepreneurial risk and a return to ingenuity. Labeling the sum of these two as "business profit," he drew a sharp distinction between entrepreneurship and capital use:

> Capital will give results, and is in the strict sense of the term capital, only if used productively; on the degree of this usefulness depends the rate of interest at which we lend capital. Productive use presupposes an industrial enterprise and an entrepreneur. The enterprise gives the entrepreneur a net yield after compensating for all expenses and costs. This net yield has two parts, business profits and capital use.
>
> (von Thünen 1960 [1850], p. 249)

H. K. von Mangoldt

A second landmark performance on the subject of the entrepreneur was produced by Hans von Mangoldt, professor at the universities of Göttingen and Freiburg. Von Mangoldt's writings remain mostly inaccessible to those unfamiliar with the German language, but we know of his contributions indirectly through Knight (1921), Schumpeter (1954), Hutchison (1953), and Hennings (1980). Knight (1921, p. 27) credits von Mangoldt with "a most careful and exhaustive analysis of profit," and Schumpeter (1954, p. 556n) judged his work on entrepreneurship "the most important advance since Say."

Von Mangoldt attempted to reform Hermann's theory, which sought the essential characteristic of entrepreneurship in the personal activity of entrepreneurs. Hermann maintained that certain kinds of labor are inseparable from the nature of entrepreneurship, and if these tasks are delegated to anyone else, the delegator ceases to be an entrepreneur. Among these tasks Hermann listed the assembling of capital, the supervision of business, the securing of credit and trade connections, and the assumption of risk connected with the prospect of irregular gains.

Von Mangoldt discarded Hermann's first three entrepreneurial tasks as inessential to a "pure" notion of entrepreneurship. He argued that although entrepreneurs customarily participate in their own enterprises with their own capital and personal supervision, these services could be furnished just as well by salaried labor. After extracting these two elements, what remains from Hermann's theory is risk-bearing. According to von Mangoldt (1907 [1855], p. 41):

> That which alone is inseparable from the concept of the entrepreneur is, on the one hand, owning the output of the undertaking – control over the product brought forth, and, on the other hand, assuming responsibility for whatever losses may occur.

Thus von Mangoldt's theory of entrepreneurship was production-oriented and risk-centered. He distinguished between "production to order" and "production for the market." The former is safe because service and payment are simultaneous, which thereby eliminates the uncertainty of changing market conditions between the start of production and sale of the final product. The latter is speculative because the product is destined for exchange on a market of uncertain demand and unknown price. Von Mangoldt (1907 [1855], p. 37) found this distinction useful, even though it is imprecise, because, strictly speaking, "every possibility of a change in the subjective estimate of the service, or the remuneration [of it], offers such an uncertainty," and "since such a possibility is excluded only by a perfect simultaneity of service and payment, every business which needs for its carrying through any time whatever, could not, in the strictest sense of the word, be undertaken to order."

This distinction therefore provides a means of discussing degrees of risk that confront the entrepreneur. By von Mangoldt's reckoning, those enterprises that require the longest time to bring their products to the point of final sale involve the most uncertainty, whereas those that involve the shortest time require the least amount of entrepreneurship. Risk and uncertainty go to the heart of the matter. The distinctiveness of the entrepreneur is that he assumes the burden of fluctuations in expenditures and revenues that mutually determine the success or failure of any enterprise. In this respect von Mangoldt stood squarely in the tradition begun by Cantillon.

Von Mangoldt also developed the notion that entrepreneurial profit is the rent of ability, and he insisted that the entrepreneur be treated as a separate factor of production. He divided entrepreneurial income into three parts: a premium on uninsurable risks; entrepreneur interest and wages, including only payments for special forms of capital or productive effort that did not admit of exploitation by anyone other than the owner; and entrepreneur rents, that is, payments for differential abilities or assets not held by anyone else. Alfred Marshall took special note of this last item, citing von Mangoldt approvingly in his development of the principle of quasi-rent.

Von Mangoldt's theory did not concentrate on an ideal type of entrepreneur but rather on the decisions he must make in an uncertain, competitive environment: the choice of techniques, the allocation of productive factors, and the marketing of production. He recognized successful innovation as part of entrepreneurship but expressed more interest in the allocative function of the entrepreneur. His contribution therefore belongs more to the static theory of resource allocation than to the dynamic theory of growth and development.

Postscript

The German tradition in political economy nurtured the concept of business leader, or *unternehmer*. Both von Thünen and von Mangoldt were important anticipators of Frank Knight (see Chapter 6), who in the next century revived Cantillon's idea of the entrepreneur as risk-bearer. In one sense, von Thünen's contribution may be judged the more significant of the two, insofar as it combined elements of risk-bearing and innovation in a way that pointed past the concept of entrepreneurship that became dominant in the next century. But Charles Tuttle (1927, p. 518) said of von Mangoldt that after his treatment, "economists could no longer consider the function [of the entrepreneur] as a mere incident to some other function, or ignore it altogether, as had been the case hitherto." And H. C. Rectenwald (1987, p. 299) adds that "Mangoldt definitely anticipates Schumpeter's theory of the entrepreneur."

5   Early neoclassical perspectives

The neoclassical era

Mark Casson (1987, p. 151) has rightly claimed that the 'disappearance' of the entrepreneur is associated with the rise of the neoclassical school of economics. Classical political economy focused on the market process, which is in many respects a discovery process: producers and sellers must discover consumer wants, resource availability, and resource costs; buyers and consumers must discover products, prices, and quality. In a discovery process, entrepreneurs have an important role in acquiring and using information.

After 1870 economic theory de-emphasized information as it turned toward the fundamental laws of price formation and resource allocation in individual markets and away from macroeconomic concerns of growth and income distribution. The deterministic models pioneered by neoclassical writers emphasized perfect information and perfect markets. The former trivializes entrepreneurial decision-making and the latter makes the entrepreneur superfluous by eliminating the coordination problem (cf. Baumol 1968). With few exceptions, economic analysis after 1870 became increasingly abstract and mechanistic. The economic problem came to be perceived as the allocation of certain scarce means among given ends, rather than the selection of the ends themselves. In this era, no longer did the great macro-economic issues of the classical period – such as population, capital supply, and economic growth – dominate economic inquiry.

The new economic analysis was developed by a breed of professional economists who, unlike their predecessors trained mostly in philosophy, received more focused training in the subject. As a sign of the "maturity" of the new discipline, which acquired separate standing as a field of study, the phrase "political economy" gradually gave way to the term "economics". The new professionals were less firmly rooted in the parent discipline of philosophy and more open to the applications of mathematics to economic reasoning.

Although the issues of the new economics were fundamentally the same, three distinct viewpoints vied for supremacy during the neoclassical era. These three approaches may be loosely identified as Austrian, French, and British. Each had a different intellectual tradition behind it, and each emphasized different things in its redirection of economic analysis. Of the three, the Austrian approach proved most fertile for advancing the theory of the entrepreneur, because it alone retained a focus on market process.

The Austrian school

With the publication of his *Principles of Economics* in 1871, Carl Menger (1840–1921) established himself as the founder and early leader of a distinctive school of economic thought that later included two able disciples, Friedrich von Wieser (1851–1926) and Eugen von Böhm-Bawerk (1851–1914). The central concern of Menger's economics was to establish the subjectivist act of human valuation as the starting point of economic theory. In the subjectivist view, economic change arises not from circumstances themselves but from an individual's awareness and understanding of them. Menger's analysis, in particular, relied heavily on the role of knowledge in individual decisions.

Although Menger's theory of production is secondary to his theory of value, we must nevertheless look to his theory of production for an appreciation of the entrepreneur. Menger's theory of production starts with the general theory of the good. For something to be a good in the economic sense requires recognition of the causal connection between a useful thing and its ability to satisfy human wants, as well as action that directs the useful thing to this satisfaction. In other words, the goods character of any useful thing is not innate; it must be acquired through human action, which requires that a person recognizes a need and strives to satisfy it.

In the Austrian framework, goods are ranked according to their causal connections. To use Menger's (1950 [1871], p. 56) example, the bread we eat, the flour from which it is baked, the grain milled into flour, and the field on which the grain is grown are all goods. But some goods serve individual needs directly and some stand in a more remote causal connection. The former are called goods of "lower order" and the latter, goods of "higher order." The further removed a good is from satisfying a want directly, the higher the number assigned to it in Menger's scale of goods-ordering. Thus bread is a good of first order because it satisfies hunger directly. Flour is a second-order good because it is one step removed from the direct satisfaction of need. The grain from which flour is milled, along with the mill and labor expended on it, are third-order goods. The field, farmers, and equipment used to grow grain are fourth-order goods, and so on.

From the foregoing we can see that to designate the order of a particular good is to indicate that in some particular employment it has a closer or more distant causal relationship with the satisfaction of a human need. For Menger, the ultimate goods character of higher-order goods depends on the power to transform goods of higher order into goods of lower order. Economic production is the process by which this transformation takes place and by which the goods of lower order are directed finally into the satisfaction of human needs. This process takes time. Over time, improvements in technology and transportation tend continually to shorten the time between phases of transforming higher-order goods into lower-order goods, but the time gaps never disappear completely. It is impossible to transform higher-order goods into lower-order goods by a mere wave of the hand. Production is never instantaneous.

Although Menger never elaborated his conception of the entrepreneur in great detail, it fits into the vision of production just outlined. According to this general theory of production, the entrepreneur is the person who handles the intertemporal coordination of the factors of production (i.e., higher-order goods). Menger recognized that industry is vertically disintegrated and that somebody has to align productive resources over time. That somebody is the entrepreneur. Ironically, the entrepreneur's own technical labor services are usually among the higher-order goods he has at his command for purposes of production. Nevertheless, it is not the supply of such services that makes one an entrepreneur; it is instead one's calculating and decision-making abilities that make one's function unique. Menger (1950 [1871], p. 160) established that entrepreneurial activity includes: (a) obtaining information about the economic situation, (b) economic calculation – all the various computations that must be made if a production process is to be efficient, (c) the act of will by which goods of higher order are assigned to a particular production process, and (d) supervising the execution of the production plan so that it may be carried through as economically as possible.

An obvious corollary of Menger's conception of entrepreneurial activity is that the entrepreneur must face uncertainty with regard to the quantity and quality of final goods he can produce by means of the higher-order goods in his possession. The degree of uncertainty faced by the entrepreneur depends on the extent of his knowledge of the productive process and upon the measure of control he exercises over it. "This uncertainty," Menger (1950 [1871], p. 71) said, "is of the greatest practical significance in human economy."

Menger did not attempt to link the entrepreneur with the capitalist; indeed it would have been a step backward for entrepreneurial theory if he had done so. But his position with regard to risk-bearing is curious, especially in the face of his repeated emphasis on the significance of uncertainty in economic affairs. Despite the fact that the entrepreneur confronts uncertainty continually in the process of production, Menger held that risk-bearing cannot be the essential function of the entrepreneur. Noting his departure from von Mangoldt on this issue, Menger (1950 [1871], p. 161) asserted that risk is insignificant to entrepreneurship, because in the final analysis the chance of loss is offset by the chance of gain.[1] Schooled in the Austrian tradition, Joseph Schumpeter (see Chapter 7) also denied risk-bearing as an essential characteristic of entrepreneurship. But in a certain sense Schumpeter stood Menger on his head. Whereas Menger saw economic progress as leading to the development of entrepreneurial activity, Schumpeter viewed entrepreneurial activity as leading to economic progress.

Friedrich von Wieser was a student of Karl Knies but a disciple of Menger. He extended Menger's ideas and added several important dimensions to his entrepreneur, among them leadership, alertness, and risk-bearing. Von Wieser (1927, p. 324) defined the entrepreneur in a "legalistic" but otherwise sweeping fashion: he claimed that the entrepreneur is the director of economic enterprise by "legal right and at the same time by virtue of his active participation in the economic management of his enterprise." Performing the various functions of legal representative, owner, employer, creditor, debtor, lessor, or lessee, the entrepreneur's:

> economic leadership commences with the establishment of the enterprise; he supplies not only the necessary capital but originates the idea, elaborates and puts into operation the plan, and engages collaborators. When the enterprise is established, he becomes its manager technically as well as commercially.
>
> (von Weiser 1927, p. 324)

Clearly, von Wieser tried to bring everything connected with the theory and practice of enterprise under his umbrella-like definition of the entrepreneur. He spoke of entrepreneurs as the "great personalities" of capitalism: "bold technical innovators, organizers with a keen knowledge of human nature, farsighted bankers, reckless speculators, the world-conquering directors of the trusts" (von Wieser 1927, p. 327). This is painting with a broad brush. Not only is von Wieser's multifarious entrepreneur required to be multi-talented, "he must [also] possess the quick perception that seizes new terms in current transactions as his affairs develop; [and] he must possess the independent forcefulness to regulate his business according to his views." Finally, he must have the courage to accept risk and be driven forward by "the joyful power to create" (von Wieser 1927, p. 324).

Von Wieser touched upon themes that would be expounded again in the next two generations of theories on entrepreneurship. Schumpeter (see Chapter 7) zeroed in on the innovating spirit and the creativity of entrepreneurs. Israel Kirzner (see Chapter 8) elaborated the perceptiveness theme. As a rule, modern theories of entrepreneurship have averted the multifarious personality of the entrepreneur in favor of a more narrowly defined figure. Eventually von Wieser admitted that institutional changes, primarily in forms of business organization, had gradually transformed the notion of entrepreneur to a mere legal concept. In the wake of such changes, von Wieser (1927, p. 328) declared: The requirement of economic management is no longer fulfilled in all cases. Today the enterprise is a voluntary community of commercial operation in the money economy subject to one entrepreneur. It may be a unified group of such operations. The entrepreneur is any legal owner of an enterprise.

The third member of the Austrian triumvirate, Eugen von Böhm-Bawerk, wrote very little about the entrepreneur, concerning himself primarily with the theory of capital and interest. Schumpeter (1954, p. 893) has alluded to von Böhm-Bawerk's uncertainty theory of profits, in which the source of entrepreneurs' profits is that things do not work out as planned. According to the theory, persistence of positive profits in a firm is a consequence of superior judgment in the face of uncertainty. We also have it on Murray Rothbard's (1985) authority that von Böhm-Bawerk clearly identified the entrepreneur with the capitalist and that he in no way suggested that they could be separated. Be that as it may, von Böhm-Bawerk did not develop his theory of profit and loss to any great extent, leaving this task to be accomplished by his student, Ludwig von Mises (see Chapter 8) and by Frank Knight (see Chapter 6).

Léon Walras

The French economist Léon Walras (1834–1910) was a leading neoclassical economist who is recognized today as the founder of general equilibrium theory. The hallmark of general equilibrium theory is the all-pervasive inter-dependence of economic affairs and markets. As developed by Walras, the theory was static rather than dynamic, but it offered, nevertheless, a limited view of economic change. Walras's economics shows us a state of ultimate and timeless adjustment maintained by the competitive self-interest of the individual suppliers of productive services. In this world each productive service contributes technically and essentially to the production, transport, and sale of goods, thereby earning each day that amount by which the withdrawal of one such productive unit would reduce the daily output of the system as a whole. Furthermore, in this analytic system the total of all the payments to the suppliers of productive services exactly exhausts their total product.

Walras's lasting contribution to economic theory was architectonic; that is, it was more a contribution of form than of substance. He constructed an elegant system of mathematical equations to represent the totality of the economic system and to emphasize the interdependence of its constituent parts. The actual numbers (i.e., coefficients) that enter these equations in specific circumstances were left for others to discover.

Outwardly Walras considered the entrepreneur an important figure. In his *Elements of Pure Economics* (1874), he carefully delineated four classes of productive factors, thus setting the mode of modern practice. His disquisition is reminiscent of Cantillon's three-class presentation of landowners, workers, and entrepreneurs, with the important difference that Walras (1954 [1874], p. 222) recognized the capitalist apart from either the landowner or the entrepreneur. He was quite explicit about the separation and distinction of economic factors of production. After dispensing with the usual categories of landowner, laborer, and capitalist, Walras wrote:

> In addition, let us designate by the term entrepreneur a fourth person, entirely distinct from those just mentioned, whose role it is to lease land from the landowner, hire personal faculties from the laborer, and borrow capital from the capitalist, in order to combine the three productive services in agriculture, industry or trade. It is undoubtedly true that, in real life, the same person may assume two, three, or even all four of the above-defined roles. In fact, the different ways in which these roles may be combined give rise to different types of enterprise. However that may be, the roles themselves, even when performed by the same individual, still remain distinct. From the scientific point of view, we must keep these roles separate and avoid both the error of the English economists who identify the entrepreneur with the capitalist and the error of a certain number of French economists who look upon the entrepreneur as a worker charged with the special task of managing a firm.

Walras's argument with the English economists concerned a point of scientific method. He argued that although in practice the functions of capitalist and entrepreneur may frequently be merged, in theory they must be treated separately in order to advance clear thinking about the nature and consequences of each. Surprisingly, he reserved his harshest criticism for his own countrymen. He accused Say of misunderstanding the very nature of the entrepreneurial function, declaring that "this person [the entrepreneur] is absent from his [Say's] theory" (Walras 1954 [1874], pp. 425–6). In view of Say's widely recognized preeminence in the history of entrepreneurial theory, this is an astounding indictment. Yet Walras justified his position by excluding the activities of coordination and supervision from the entrepreneur's functions. Those activities, he argued repeatedly, are part of routine management and are therefore rewarded by the payment of the wages of management (cf. Walker 1986, p. 5).[2]

A study of Walras's correspondence shows that he maintained his position on the entrepreneur consistently over a long period of time. In his *Elements*, first published in 1874, he characterized the entrepreneur as an intermediary between production and consumption, an equilibrating agent egged on by profit opportunities in the marketplace. Profit opportunities exist whenever selling price is greater than costs of production. Thus it would appear that the entrepreneur operates in an arena of disequilibrium. Walras (1954 [1874], p. 225) described how the entrepreneur adjusts supplies in line with manifest demands in a manner evocative of Cantillon:

> [I]f the selling price of a product exceeds the cost of the productive services for certain firms and a profit results, entrepreneurs will flow towards this branch of production or expand their output, so that the quantity of the product [on the market] will increase, its price fall, and the difference between price and cost will be reduced; and, if [on the contrary], the cost of the productive services exceeds the selling price for certain firms, so that a loss results, entrepreneurs will leave this branch of production or curtail their output, so that the quantity of the product [on the market] will decrease, its price will rise and the difference between price and cost will again be reduced.

In 1887 Walras (1965, vol. 2, p. 212) wrote to the American economist Francis Walker that "The definition of the entrepreneur is, in my opinion, the thing that binds all of economics together." He persistently argued against the admixture of economic functions, declaring the entrepreneur to be "exclusively ... the person who buys productive services on the market for services and sells products on the market for products, thus obtaining either a profit or a loss."

> Walras repeated his position on the entrepreneur several years later in a letter to his disciple Vilfredo Pareto, explaining how he differed from Alfred Marshall on the subject: Marshall reasons mainly by assumption that the owner of services is a worker who takes it upon himself to make goods and sell them," whereas, "I interpose the entrepreneur as a distinct person whose role is essentially that of demanding services and selling products.
>
> (Walras 1965, vol. 2, p. 629)

We may take this evidence as confirmation of the fact that the entrepreneur held a prominent place in Walras's view of the world as it actually operates. The extent to which he integrated the function of the entrepreneur into the core of his analytical system is another matter, however. At issue is the idealized nature of Walras's theoretic model and whether it bears any resemblance to real-world practice. William Jaffé, a leading Walrasian scholar, and to a lesser extent Schumpeter, an avowed admirer of Walras, occupy one extreme in this debate. Michio Morishima and Donald Walker occupy the opposite extreme.

Walras himself obscured matters by introducing the "zero-profit entrepreneur" into his static general equilibrium system, a model devoid of time or uncertainty. Since the entrepreneur neither gains nor loses in competitive equilibrium, his *raison d'être* disappears in that state. In order to arrive at a determinate mathematical solution, Walras expunged all of the things from his model that gave meaning to the entrepreneur. Mathematical nicety and practical necessity inevitably clashed, and Walras was not able to reconcile the two. This explains why there are very few mathematical models that formally analyze entrepreneurial behavior within a closed economic system. Enmeshed in this dilemma and seeing no way out, Walras developed a theoretic construct of an economy that worked like a predictable, impersonal, and frictionless machine. In G. L. S. Shackle's phrase, it was an "inhuman model," incapable of conveying the full range of economic activity (Shackle 1955, p. 91). On this account, Schumpeter (1954, p. 893) concluded that Walras's contribution to the theory of entrepreneurship was essentially negative.

Morishima (1977) defended Walras by reasserting the centrality of the entrepreneur in Walras's theoretic model, but he was roundly criticized by Jaffé (1980, p. 535), who insisted that "In his whole theoretical construct, Walras deliberately abstracted from uncertainty." This explains the absence of the entrepreneur, *qua* entrepreneur, from the Walrasian model in its "normal" operation. Jaffé (1980, pp. 529–30) concluded that "As for the role of the entrepreneur in Walras's analytical model, the *Elements* restricted it to that of arbitrageur, and nothing else." But Jaffé's position has been challenged by his former student Donald Walker (1986, p. 18), who asserts that Walras made important and lasting contributions to the theory of the entrepreneur and that Schumpeter built his own novel concept of the entrepreneur on a Walrasian foundation.

Thus diversity of opinion continues to beset Walras's contribution to the theory of entrepreneurship. On the one hand it appears that Walras had an unambiguous notion of real-world entrepreneurs and that he assigned them great importance in the practical world of business. But on the other hand his chief scientific achievement, the mathematical general equilibrium model, systematically eliminated – by assumption (and perhaps by necessity) – the centrality of the entrepreneur.[3] As theory goes, Walras's general equilibrium system was a momentous contribution. But as a suitable showcase for the essentiality of the entrepreneur it was a total void.

Alfred Marshall and his disciples

In an earlier chapter we showed how the English variant of classical economics (Smith–Ricardo–Mill) tended to conflate the roles of capitalist and entrepreneur. For its part, British neoclassical value theory did not develop a theory of enterprise, and only grudgingly did it yield a theory of capital. Consequently, the introduction of marginal utility theory did not limit the range of possible differences of opinion concerning the entrepreneur. The new economics took ends as given, explained allocation of scarce resources to meet these given ends, and focused attention on equilibrium results rather than on adjustment processes. It therefore left little or no room for entrepreneurial action. The entrepreneur became a mere automaton, a passive onlooker with no real scope for individual decision-making. Certain British writers kept the concept alive, however, so that at least *sub rosa*, the entrepreneur remained in economic theory.

The leading British economist at the turn of the century was Alfred Marshall (1842–1924), who built a durable bridge between classical and neoclassical economics. Marshall dominated British theoretical economics and its pedagogy for a generation (1890 to 1920). His approach to the meaning and function of the "undertaker" and the "business leader" was influenced by the principles of biological evolution expounded by Darwin and Wallace. The peculiar skill and ability of the entrepreneur, Marshall argued, are shaped by an economic struggle for survival in the competitive marketplace.

Marshall elaborated a concept of entrepreneurship that is rooted in the writings of Say and Mill but is more expansive than either's theory. The core of his concept remained steadfast, but at the periphery its facets evolved over time. Marshall (1920b, p. 356, 358) described the elements of "business genius" as alertness, sense of proportion, strength of reasoning, coordination, innovation, and willingness to take risks. He argued that this combination of abilities could be acquired through experience but not taught by formal education.

In his writings Marshall reserved a special place for the human agent that directs rather than follows economic circumstances. He divided entrepreneurs into two classes: active and passive. Active entrepreneurs are "those who open out new and improved methods of business," whereas passive entrepreneurs are "those who follow beaten tracks" (Marshall

1920a, p. 597). He made it clear that entrepreneurs of the latter group receive "wages of superintendence," but he carefully elaborated the elements of superintendence so as to add greater substance to Mill's notion of entrepreneurship. However, he reserved his main attention for the active entrepreneur, whose reward is subject to risk. The venturesome entrepreneur cannot avoid risk, because he directs capital and labor to an uncertain end. In order to be successful, therefore, he must be capable of conceiving "wise and far reaching policies, and … carry[ing] them out calmly and resolutely" (Marshall 1920a, p. 606).

At bottom, Marshall's entrepreneur was a business manager, although he used the term management to mean more than mere superintendence. Following Darwin, Marshall argued that professional business managers emerge as a special group from an evolutionary process that is driven by specialization and division of labor. This "Darwinism" may explain Marshall's inability or unwillingness to tie the entrepreneur to a single function or set of abilities. The concept itself seems to evolve endlessly in Marshall's writings, but in the final analysis, he placed more emphasis on the existence and necessity of business ability than on anything else.[4]

In his early work, Marshall stressed duty as an important stimulus to human action. But his faith in the widespread application of this Victorian virtue dwindled during the 1880s. After 1890 Marshall placed the chief responsibility for the economic and moral progress of society on the restless, farsighted, pioneering, but unsung entrepreneur. By 1907 duty had receded further into the background, and Marshall (1925, pp. 332–3) was extolling the entrepreneur for his imagination as well as his leadership:

> Men of this class live in constantly shifting visions, fashioned in their own brains, of various routes to their desired end; of the difficulties which nature will oppose to them on each route, and of the contrivances by which they hope to get the better of her opposition. This imagination gains little credit with the people, because it is not allowed to run riot; its strength is disciplined by a stronger will; and its highest glory is to have attained great ends by means so simple that no one will know, and none but experts will even guess, how a dozen other expedients, each suggesting as much brilliancy to the hasty observer, were set aside in favour of it.

In a purely analytical sense, the most important contribution Marshall made to the theory of entrepreneurship was to extend von Mangoldt's notion of rent-of-ability, though he did not, as Schumpeter (1954, p. 894) points out, restrict the idea to the entrepreneur. Freeing himself from the analytical impediments of the classical wages-fund doctrine, Marshall attempted to cut through the amorphous nature of "labor" to capture the uniqueness of individual ability. Observation and experience told him that "business genius" was unevenly distributed and that unique skills received a kind of surplus or rent. But he sometimes treated entrepreneurs as members of a class and sometimes as individuals. According to Marshall (1920a, p. 623):

> [T]he class of business undertakers contains a disproportionately large number of persons with high natural ability; since, in addition to the able men born within its ranks it includes also a large share of the best natural abilities born in the lower ranks of industry. And thus while profits on capital invested in education is a specially important element in the incomes of professional men taken as a class, the rent of rare natural abilities may be regarded as a specially important element in the income of business men, so long as we consider them as individuals.

Marshall's tendency to speak of entrepreneurs sometimes as a class and sometimes as individuals has not helped the cause of clear thinking on the subject. For example, Frederick Harbison asserts that Marshall's notion of the entrepreneur applies not to a single individual but rather to a hierarchy of individuals. Thus he argues that the Marshallian entrepreneur is essentially "an organization which comprises all of the people required to perform entrepreneurial functions" (Harbison 1956, p. 356). We find it difficult to reconcile this interpretation with the idea of the entrepreneur as a person of unique abilities who receives a quasi-rent, insofar as quasi-rents can only be ascertained for individuals, and any aggregation of these magnitudes seems specious at best.

Despite the fact that Marshall wrote during the high tide of competitive capitalism, his theory of entrepreneurship gave little prominence to invention and innovation (Shove 1942). Also, despite his lip service to evolution as a vital force in economics, he devoted his intellectual energies mainly to advancing the theory of comparative statics and partial equilibrium. For the most part, his students and disciples followed suit.

Francis Y. Edgeworth (1845–1926), a disciple of Marshall and an important neoclassical economist in his own right, recognized the importance of the entrepreneur but added no new dimensions to the concept. Initially, Edgeworth (1925, vol. 1, p. 16) raised the proverbial question "What is an entrepreneur?" By way of answering, he reviewed the four "type-specimens" promulgated, in turn, by (1) the classical economists (i.e., the entrepreneur as capitalist), (2) F. A. Walker (i.e., the entrepreneur as non-capitalist employer), (3) F. B. Hawley (i.e., the entrepreneur as risk-taker), and (4) Léon Walras (i.e., the entrepreneur who makes no profit). Unfortunately, he neither reduced the list to a single definition nor attempted a workable synthesis. Instead, Edgeworth suggested that the choice of definition is dictated by the type of economic inquiry undertaken. But he registered his objection to the zero-profit entrepreneur, regardless of whether this creature follows Walras's or Walker's construction.

Edgeworth returned to the issue of the zero-profit entrepreneur several years later in a sustained attempt to defend Marshall's version of the entrepreneur against the "errors" of Walras. The real debate, however, was not about the action and significance of the entrepreneur; it was about the reward for the entrepreneur's effort. Edgeworth acknowledged Walras's contribution but rejected his conclusion as paradoxical and unsound. Ostensibly Edgeworth shared Walras's definition of the entrepreneur as a buyer of services and a seller of products. But he did not understand Walras's notion of profits. He speaks, therefore, of the entrepreneur's remuneration in terms of wages and interest (i.e., Marshallian profits). Walras (1965, vol. 2, p. 629) maintained that in equilibrium the entrepreneur would receive no profit as entrepreneur, but that he would get non-entrepreneurial income in the form of interest, rent, or (managerial) wages. Thus Edgeworth's attack on the "paradoxical" notion of the zero-profit entrepreneur was based on a misunderstanding of the nature of Walrasian profits and was therefore wide of the mark. Finally, Edgeworth was unable to complete satisfactorily the analysis of income distribution by partitioning the entrepreneur from the other factors. "To determine at what point the capitalist ends and the entrepreneur begins," he wrote, "appears to defy analysis" (Edgeworth 1925, vol. 1, p. 48).

Marshall's successor at Cambridge was A. C. Pigou (1877–1959). Pigou also took up the subject of the entrepreneur, but he was less interested in the theory of distribution than in the macroeconomic consequences of the entrepreneur's activities. From a microeconomic standpoint, his view of the entrepreneur was passive and unenlightening. He saw the entrepreneur as an owner and a broker, merely one link in the economic chain that connects production and distribution. "The entrepreneurs," he wrote simply, "by whom the stream of goods that comes to completion every year is legally owned, sell these goods for money to wholesale houses and shopkeepers" (Pigou 1929, p. 132).

When he turned to the macroeconomy, however, Pigou emphasized the element of uncertainty, which has an impact on industrial fluctuations because of its effect on entrepreneurs' decisions. "Business men in making [production] forecasts are shadowed by immense uncertainties," he said; and the "immediate cause lying behind general movements of employment consists in shifts in the expectation of business men about future prospects, or, if we prefer a looser term, business confidence" (Pigou 1949, p. 216).

British thinking on the subject of the entrepreneur developed little in the generation after Marshall, an era that came to be dominated by Marshall's brilliant student John Maynard Keynes (1883–1946). Keynes treated the concept rather perfunctorily, retaining some basic notions of the entrepreneur as financier and employer – the residual claimant of profit. Like Marshall, Keynes placed the entrepreneur in the role of decision-maker within the individual firm, proclaiming that his function is to "fix the amount of employment at that level which [is] expect[ed] to maximize the excess of the proceeds over the factor costs" (Keynes 1964, p. 25).

As an active factor of production, the entrepreneur must confront uncertainty in his attempts to forecast "effective demand." The significance of uncertainty in the Keynesian paradigm has generally been understated by all but a few of Keynes's disciples, yet in many respects it was his most revolutionary contribution. The well-worn story in the history of economic thought is that Keynes's concern with macroeconomic variables subsequently shifted economists' attention away from the entrepreneur and toward the performance of certain aggregates in the economy. However true this may be, there is another side to *The General Theory of Employment, Interest, and Money*. Keynes's focus on uncertainty in decision-making, and more generally on expectations, provides a link between Marshall's notion of "the entrepreneur as manager" and the contemporary theory of enterprise and radical uncertainty advanced, for example, by G. L. S. Shackle, a disciple of Keynes (see Chapter 8).

Be that as it may, Keynes' discussion of the animus behind entrepreneurial activity is distinctly uneconomic and must be approached with caution. His comment on the nature of the uncertainty faced by entrepreneurs is that "Businessmen play a mixed game of skill and chance, the average results of which to the players are not known by those who take a hand" (Keynes 1964, p. 150). This statement is innocuous enough, but in its wake Keynes did something extraordinary. He linked enterprise not to calculations of expected profit alone but to "animal spirits" – the spontaneous urge to action that Keynes declared to be innate in the human psyche. Keynes hardly gave precise meaning to this phrase, and one rarely encounters it in subsequent treatments of the entrepreneur. He was obviously keen to insert psychological traits into the discussion.

> It is safe to say that enterprise which depends on hopes stretching into the future benefits the community as a whole. But individual initiative will only be adequate when reasonable calculation is supplemented and supported by animal spirits, so that the thought of ultimate loss which overtakes pioneers, as experience undoubtedly tells us and them, is put aside as a healthy man puts aside the expectation of death.
>
> (Keynes 1964, p. 161)

In the final analysis, Keynes' explanation of entrepreneurial activity rests as much on whim, sentiment, or chance as it does on rational expectations of profit opportunities. Psychologically this may be on the mark, but from an analytical standpoint, it is a dead end.

Postscript

Among the neoclassical writers, French thinking followed Walras toward a mechanistic market model that tended to squeeze out the entrepreneur. Neoclassical British writers never seemed to escape the kind of strait-jacket that was bequeathed to them by the Smith–Ricardo–Mill tradition. Only the Austrians advanced the theory of the entrepreneur in a substantial way as the nineteenth century drew to a close. Their analysis of the subject bore fruit in the later work of Ludwig von Mises and Joseph Schumpeter, who were schooled in the Austrian tradition.

6   The view from America

With the Civil War behind it in 1865, the United States began a period of recovery and reconstruction. This era produced little in the way of leading economists, as American intellectuals looked to Europe for stimulation and guidance. Lacking an extensive pedigree in graduate education, the new nation sent many of its leading intellectuals to Germany for advanced training. But as the nineteenth century drew to a close, American economists began to emerge from the shadows of European influence and assert themselves more independently. Not surprisingly given the country's rise from colonial status to full-fledged market economy, economists in the United States revealed a lively and ongoing interest in the place of the entrepreneur within economic theory. From the outset U.S. economists improved upon the English treatment by insisting that the entrepreneur be separated from the capitalist. Thomas Cochran (1968) attributes this fact to the early development of modern corporations in the United States. But in all likelihood this theoretic turn was also affected by a pervasive German influence on U.S. scholars, many of whom received postgraduate economics degrees in that country.

Amasa Walker and Francis A. Walker

As early as 1866, Amasa Walker (1799–1875) of Amherst College lamented the confusion in English political economy between the capitalist and the entrepreneur. Walker recognized the important role of the entrepreneur in creating economic wealth, but his discussion of this special resource did not range beyond the act of production. He defined the entrepreneur simply as one who brings about "an advantageous union between labor and capital," and he identified this special agent variously as employer, manager, entrepreneur, projector, contractor, businessman, merchant, farmer, or "whatever else he may be called, whose services are indispensable" (Walker 1866, p. 279).[1] Although he called the reward of entrepreneurial effort "profit,"

Walker offered no real distinction between the reward to the entrepreneur and the return to labor. "Profits are merely wages received by the employer (entrepreneur)," he declared, and as such, they are regulated by supply and demand.

Ultimately, Walker traded one confusion (entrepreneur-as-capitalist) for another (entrepreneur-as-worker). However, he also hinted at the notion of profit as a scarcity rent, an idea that his son, Francis Amasa Walker (1840–97), later seized on and expanded into a unique theory of profits. Amasa Walker (1866, p. 285) noted that entrepreneurs, like workers, will experience a rise or fall in their remuneration depending on whether there is excess demand for, or excess supply of, their services:

> If there are too many competing for profits, the rate will fall until the excess is driven back into the ranks of labor. As there are, however, comparatively few, in proportion to the whole number of persons capable of labor, who have the requisite capacity and training required for transacting business successfully, and fewer still who can command the necessary means of capital, it will follow that the rewards of the employer will be larger than those of the persons employed.

Amasa Walker's son, Francis, rose to the rank of general in the Civil War; later he became president of the Massachusetts Institute of Technology and served as the first president of the American Economics Association. He emphasized the fact that the entrepreneur, as distinct from the capitalist, is the chief agent of production. Like his father, he depicted the entrepreneur as an employer of other economic resources. Declaring that French economists since Say had been on the right track, he criticized English and U.S. economists who depicted the capitalist as the employer of labor merely by the fact that he possesses capital. Walker's clearest description of the entrepreneur's function is contained in *The Wages Question*, where he declared that the entrepreneur's role is "to furnish technical skills, commercial knowledge, and powers of administration; to assume responsibilities and provide against contingencies; to shape and direct production, and to organize and control the industrial machine" (Walker 1876, p. 245).

Francis Walker allied himself with the French economists in terms of his theory of income distribution (1884, p. 203), but he also declared its affinity with Marshall's theory (1887, p. 275). Like Marshall, Walker maintained that profit is the return to the differential skill and talent of practicing entrepreneurs. In other words, it is in the nature of a rent. "The term wages cannot be applied thereto," Walker (1884, p. 204) declared, "without inducing a wholly unnecessary and mischievous confusion of ideas, leading directly to false results."

Like Marshall, Walker realized that the successful conduct of business under free and active competition depends upon exceptional abilities or exceptional opportunities (the former dominated his thinking). Both writers recognized as well that these abilities are not equally distributed throughout mankind, just as land of equal fertility is not uniformly distributed over geographic space. Successful entrepreneurs have the power of foresight, a facility for organization and administration, unusual energy, and other leadership qualities – traits that are generally in short supply. By analogy, profit is due to differential ability, just as land rent is due to differential fertility (or differential location).

Focusing on the analogy between rents and profits, Walker contemplated a theoretical, no-profits stage of production. Assuming a homogeneous supply of entrepreneurs (clearly distinguished from non-entrepreneurs) sufficient to meet demand, Walker (1884, p. 207) asserted that either the entrepreneurs would combine to create a monopoly price for their services, "which is altogether improbable, or, else, they would, by competing among themselves for the amount of business, bring down its rate to so low a point that the remuneration of no one of this class would exceed what he could earn for himself in other avocations." This "no-profits" stage of production, Walker asserted, is directly analogous to the "no-rent" stage of land cultivation. Consequently, he concluded that profits form no part of the price of manufactured products, any more than rent constitutes a part of the price of agricultural commodities (as Ricardo had argued).

In recognition of the random distribution of entrepreneurial talent across populations, Walker identified four levels of entrepreneurs, each distinguished by its degree of qualifications:

> First, we have those rarely-gifted persons … whose commercial dealings have the air of magic; who have such power of foresight; who are so resolute and firm in temper that apprehensions and alarms and repeated shocks of disaster never cause them to relax their hold or change their course; who have such command over men that all with whom they have to do acquire vigor from the contact.

Next, in descending order, is a second class of high-ordered talent, persons of "natural mastery, sagacious, prompt and resolute in their avocations"; followed by a third class of those who do reasonably well in business, although more by diligence than by genius; and finally, the fourth group of ne'er-do-wells of the "zero-profit" class, those:

> of checkered fortunes, sometimes doing well, but more often ill; men who are in business because they have forced themselves into it under a

mistaken idea of their own abilities, perhaps encouraged by the partiality
of friends who have been willing to place in their hands the agencies of
production, or intrust them with commercial or banking capital.

(Walker 1884, pp. 208–9)

Except for the different gradations of entrepreneurs, it should be noted that
the view of profit as a return to differential abilities was not original with
Walker. We have seen that von Mangoldt sketched the outlines of the theory
decades earlier and that Marshall upheld the concept. In fact, it is curious that
Walker aligned himself with the French economists in this matter, insofar as
his theory had a greater affinity with that of von Mangoldt, who represented
a more familiar German tradition.

Frederick Hawley and John Bates Clark

Another U.S. economist who insisted on the functional separation of entrepreneur and capitalist was Frederick B. Hawley (1843–1929). Hawley had
a background in cotton brokerage and the lumber business. He was a keen
student of classical economics, but he was also a fiercely independent thinker
who made up his own mind on analytic issues. His confrontation with von
Böhm-Bawerk's theory of capital and interest led him to undertake a more
intense study of entrepreneurship. Hawley (1892, p. 281) firmly believed
that it is impossible to understand why capital has a price unless "we study
industrial phenomena from the undertaker's point of view."

In a series of turn-of-the-century articles in the *Quarterly Journal of
Economics*, Hawley established a risk theory of profit that he set against
von Böhm-Bawerk's theory. He equated enterprise with risk-taking and
characterized the entrepreneur as the great dynamic force of a capitalist
economy. Stressing risk and uncertainty, Hawley ranked enterprise with
land, labor, and capital as the four fundamental productive factors. He
regarded risk and uncertainty as commonplace in the industrial system.
Hawley claimed that final consumers must pay for the risk entailed in every
industrial undertaking, whether or not capital is involved. "And the reason
is this: that everybody except the gambler – everybody, that is, engaged in
industry – prefers a certainty to an uncertainty" (Hawley 1892, p. 285).

Here again we find a bonding of entrepreneurship and uncertainty reminiscent of Cantillon's early treatment. Although Hawley was apparently
unaware of Cantillon's performance, he echoed the phrases of his predeces-
sor. The special peculiarity of every business risk, Hawley (1893, p. 464)
asserted, is nothing more than "the uncertainty of how the selling price of an
unsold product will compare with the cost, or how the cost of an unfinished
product will compare with the selling price, if the latter has been agreed

upon."[2] There is a slight Benthamite strain to Hawley's argument because he recognized that some elements of cost could be fixed through insurance. But it was John Bates Clark (1847–1938) who made Hawley aware of the distinction between insurable and uninsurable risk.

Hawley's ideas on entrepreneurship were provocative enough to spark a lively debate with Clark, who was the preeminent American economist at the turn of the century. Clark (1892, p. 40) acknowledged that Hawley and von Mangoldt were correct in asserting that "Men do not hazard their capital for an amount of annual gains that in a long term of years will just offset their losses. They demand more than this and they get it." However, Clark refused to concede that risk-bearing was an entrepreneurial activity. He argued, as Schumpeter did at a later date, that all risk is borne by the capitalist.

Clark (1892, pp. 45–6) used the term entrepreneur "in an unusually strict sense, to designate the man who coordinates capital and labor without in his own proper capacity furnishing either of them." It was his view that "the entrepreneur, as such, is empty-handed," a phrase evocative of Israel Kirzner's "pure and penniless entrepreneur." In other words, the entrepreneur cannot risk anything, because he has nothing to risk.

In later works Clark couched his discussion in terms of statics and dynamics, giving support to the distinction that inclined Schumpeter to a more dynamic view of entrepreneurship. In Clark's analysis the static state is a situation where demand, capital, and technology are given. Static conditions do change over time, however: populations grow, wants change, and improved production technologies are discovered and implemented. But in Clark's world, departures from static-state equilibria are evolutionary. The mobility of labor and capital is requisite to the restoration of new, albeit temporary, equilibria.

In the dynamic economy Clark made the entrepreneur responsible for the coordination that restores the economy to an equilibrium position.[3] According to Clark (1907, pp. 82–3), this coordinator (entrepreneur) may perform several functions:

> He may, for example, both labor and furnish capital, and he may, further, perform a special coordinating function which is not labor, in the technical sense, and scarcely involves any continuous personal activity at all, but is essential for rendering labor and capital productive.

This notion of the entrepreneur as the dynamic force that moves the economy back to equilibrium after some disturbance is still very much alive in contemporary theory, but it was soon to be challenged by Schumpeter's counter-claim that the entrepreneur is the agent that *causes* disequilibrium. On the related matter of insurance, Clark (1892) recognized the differences between insurable and uninsurable risks (which he termed "static" and "dynamic"), but he did not go so far as to integrate this distinction into a general theory that based profit on risk as well as dynamic change.

Hawley offered two rejoinders to Clark's criticism, one in 1893 and a summary statement seven years later designed to answer Clark and other intervening critics. In the second rejoinder Hawley (1900, p. 78) advanced the view that "all individual incomes are composite, and that it is hard to imagine one that does not contain an element of profit and loss, as there is an element of uncertainty in the income of everybody." In its time this was an unorthodox view because it went against the prevailing tendency to compartmentalize distributional returns to factors of production. Yet it was particularly stimulating to academic economists who stubbornly resisted the idea that the theory of enterprise was a dark corner of economics that hid nothing of real importance.

Herbert Davenport and Frank Taussig

The theme that engaged Hawley in the 1890s was picked up again by Frank Knight in the 1920s and expanded into a more robust theory of risk, uncertainty, and profit. But before Knight's harvest, two other writers sowed the field. In a much-neglected book entitled *The Economics of Enterprise* (1913), Herbert J. Davenport (1861–1931) unveiled the first carefully orchestrated and sustained attempt to understand economics from the point of view of the entrepreneur. Like his teacher Thorstein Veblen, Davenport was considered something of a maverick and iconoclast. His book created a minor furor. Frank A. Fetter (1914, p. 555), a leading contemporary, denounced it as radical and unsound, which may account for its comparative neglect thereafter.

While Fetter ranted about Davenport's "riotous rhetoric" and offbeat examples, he failed utterly to confront the genuine uniqueness of the book – its concerted attempt to reorient economics from the entrepreneur's point of view.[4] Davenport held that economics consists of analyzing and explaining the actions of entrepreneurs. "We live in a society organized under competitive entrepreneur production," he declared, and on this axiomatic base he attempted to reconstruct economic theory. The fact that he did not succeed totally does not lessen the value of his attempt.

The Economics of Enterprise is a general treatise, purporting to explain production and distribution as well as the roles of money and credit. It is about competitive economics and its distinguishing characteristic, price formation. Davenport's analysis bears certain imprints of the Austrian school, such as methodological individualism, emphasis on causal sequences (1913, pp. 110–11), recognition of elements of time preference (1913, pp. 219–22), the significance of opportunity costs (1913, pp. 62–3), and the necessity of decision-making under uncertainty (1913, p. 74).

Davenport (1913, p. 140) made the entrepreneur the pivotal figure in the competitive price regime, adopting the Walrasian perspective that "the entrepreneur is a buyer of services and a seller of their products." He also proclaimed that "The entrepreneur is the independent, unemployed manager; the one who carries the risks and claims the gains of the enterprise" (Davenport 1913, p. 67). Doing Cantillon one turn better, Davenport argued that the entrepreneur faces uncertain costs as well as uncertain sales prices. The entrepreneur's true costs are uncertain for various reasons (some exogenous), but chief among them is the indeterminacy of his opportunity costs. Rather than be frozen in inactivity by uncertainty, however, it is the nature of the entrepreneur to hazard a guess and to get on with it. Thus the entrepreneur:

> estimates and surmises and hazards where he cannot know, and as a sort of general summary, setting many things over against many others, he decides upon his line of largest net advantage, making often not better than a rough guess, but none the less, a decision.
>
> (Davenport 1913, p. 74)

Cantillon told us long ago that the entrepreneur adjusts supplies in line with demand. Davenport went into greater detail. He said that entrepreneurs adjust relative supplies, each by working out his individual cost computations, including opportunity costs. These costs are themselves the manifestation of the fundamental relations of demand and relative scarcity. He made it clear that the entrepreneur does not determine prices. However, it is necessary to study the causes of price from the entrepreneur's point of view, he argued, because "it is through the entrepreneur process that the ultimate causes are forced to obtain expression in a competitive society" (Davenport 1913, p. 109). This viewpoint puts him at odds with later writers such as Ronald Coase, Kenneth Arrow, and Oliver Williamson, who take the existence of markets as a starting point and theorize that, in an ideal world, the price system can and will do everything, with no need of entrepreneurship.

Davenport was careful always to distinguish between the man of science (e.g., the economist) and the man of action (e.g., the entrepreneur). Despite the subjective and uncertain nature of economic costs, Davenport (1913, pp. 74–5) asserted that the task of the entrepreneur is relatively simple. He makes decisions based on calculations as best he can, taking the imperfect nature of the information that confronts him. He does not concern himself with things he cannot change; he merely adjusts to them. To do otherwise would "waste his energies as an entrepreneur" and make of him a "mere scientist."

According to Davenport, the degree and direction of entrepreneurial activity are dictated by costs and by prospective demand. He did not suggest that the entrepreneur engages in anything like "creative destruction," to use Schumpeter's term (see Chapter 7). Rather the entrepreneur's role is to oversee the competitive market process, which is made intelligible through the interaction of demand and supply. Davenport hinted at the pervasiveness of entrepreneurial activity while emphasizing the elements of direction and supervision. "In the main," he wrote, the price "process is captained by the entrepreneur, is guided and supervised by him, and worked out through him." Moreover, "All employers of labor or of instrumental goods for hire are entrepreneurs, no matter whether the prospective product is to be offered for sale or not" (Davenport 1913, p. 139).

In the final analysis, Davenport's entrepreneur, like Walker's, is an employer of the other factors of production. His reward, in Davenport's view, should properly be considered a subcategory of wages. Strictly speaking, profit is neither a return to risk nor a payment for the labor of superintendence. It is a payment "to the entrepreneur for entrepreneur activity as such. This profit goes, truly, to him who takes the risk, but does not, therefore, go as compensation for the risk or in proportion to it" (Davenport 1908, p. 98).

By denying risk-bearing as an entrepreneurial activity, Davenport aligned himself with Clark. Yet he rejected Clark's marginal productivity theory of distribution on the grounds that it requires information that is unobtainable, even by the wisest entrepreneur. In practice, entrepreneurs are limited in terms of their ability to assess the precise contributions of other agents of production. Davenport (1913, p. 148) concluded that about all the entrepreneur can do is:

> to attribute to each factor a degree of serviceability for his ends commensurate with what he has to pay for it and to treat whatever is left as due to his own personal activity in the quest for gain. But this is crude in theory; his profit is partly due to the fact that he is able to make an intermediate good or agent signify more to him than he has to pay for it in wages or rent.

Frank W. Taussig (1859–1940), of Harvard University, reprised Davenport's claim that profit is a subcategory of wages, but he also characterized the entrepreneur as a residual claimant, which explains the irregularity of his income (Taussig 1915, p. 159). Taussig's entrepreneur guides and directs economic activity. He is a multifaceted individual, but above all, he requires imagination and judgment (Taussig 1915, p. 163). Differential abilities do exist and are unevenly distributed among businessmen, according to Taussig

(1915, p. 175), but he insisted that Walker's "rent-theory" of profits cannot explain the fundamentals of profit, only the differences in profits among entrepreneurs.[5]

Taussig flirted with the Schumpeterian notion of the innovative entrepreneur as the singular architect of economic progress. He recognized that in a static world of perfect competition the managers of industry would receive nothing but wages, which would be determined in the same manner as other payments for labor.

> But in a dynamic state – a state of unstable equilibrium, of transition, of advance – there is opportunity for businessmen to secure something more. By taking the lead in utilizing inventions or improving organization they make extra gains, which last so long as they succeed in holding the lead. Business profits, so considered, are ever vanishing, ever reappearing. They are the stimulus to improvement and the reward for improvement, tending to cease once the improvement is fully applied.
>
> (Taussig 1915, p. 185)

Taussig studied in Berlin, so he obviously read German. Schumpeter's *Theory of Economic Development* appeared in German in 1912 but was not translated to English until 1934. Although the timing is fortuitous, it is not clear that Schumpeter had any influence on Taussig. Despite some Schumpeter-like phrases, Taussig could not totally break the link between profits and wages in his own mind. He maintained that a sharp separation of business profits from wages is artificial:

> Even the routine conduct of established industries calls for judgment and administrative capacity, and so for the exercise of the same faculties that are more conspicuously and more profitably exercised under conditions of rapid progress. To separate even roughly the earnings of a successful business man into two parts – one wages, the other 'profits' in the sense of gains from progress – would seem to be quite impracticable. Looking over the whole varied range of earnings among those engaged in the business career, it is simplest to regard them all as returns to labor, – returns marked by many peculiarities, among which the most striking are the risks and uncertainties, the wide range, the high gains from able pioneering.
>
> (Taussig 1915, p. 185)

In the final analysis, Taussig held that although innovation is one of the activities that may be performed by the entrepreneur, it is not the only one and probably not even the most important one. Rarely, he asserted, do the requisite business qualities and inventive traits reside in the same person (Taussig 1915, p. 164).

Frank Knight

Of all the American writers, the one to whom we owe the fullest and most careful examination of the role of the entrepreneur is Frank Knight (1885–1972), whose contribution was twofold. First, he provided a very useful emphasis on the distinction between insurable risks and non-insurable uncertainty. Second, he advanced a theory of profit that related this non-insurable uncertainty on the one hand to rapid economic change and on the other to differences in entrepreneurial ability. In so doing Knight established a meaningful synthesis of the Hawley–Clark formulations.

Knight charged that previous "risk theories" were ambiguous because they did not distinguish sufficiently between two very different kinds of risk. On the one hand, risk signifies a quantity capable of being measured – that is, the objective probability that an event will happen. Because this kind of risk can be shifted from the entrepreneur to another party by an insurance contract, it is not an uncertainty in any meaningful sense. On the other hand, "risk" is often taken to mean an immeasurable eventuality, such as the inability to predict consumer demand. Knight dubbed the latter "true" uncertainty and geared his theories of profit and entrepreneurship to its magnitude. The best summary statement of this theory comes from Knight himself:

> [N]ot all "risks" necessarily give rise to profit, or loss. Many kinds can be insured against, which eliminates them as factors of uncertainty. ... The essential point for profit theory is that insofar as it is possible to insure by any method against risk, the cost of carrying it is converted into a constant element of expense, and it ceases to be a cause of profit and loss. The uncertainties which persist as causes of profit are those which are uninsurable because there is no objective measure of the probability of gain or loss. This is true especially of the prediction of demand. It not only cannot be foreseen accurately, but there is no basis for saying that the probability of its being of one sort rather than another is of a certain value – as we can compute the chance that a man will live to a certain age. Situations in regard to which business judgment must be exercised do not repeat themselves with sufficient conformity to type to make possible a computation of probability.
>
> (Knight 1951, pp. 119–20)

Modern practice has refined Knight's distinction in the following way. Things once considered uninsurable because of lack of a measurable probability distribution have, in fact, been insured. Recent literature therefore makes three distinctions where Knight made two. Risk refers to the situation where the probability distribution of possible outcomes is calculable and known. Uncertainty refers to a situation where the possible outcomes are identifiable but the probability distribution of outcomes is not known. Radical uncertainty refers to a situation in which the possible outcomes of a given event are unknown and unknowable.

By isolating the concept of risk and refining its meaning, Knight gave new clarity to Cantillon's theory of the entrepreneur as the bearer of uncertainty. He also attributed the evolutionary nature of enterprise organizations to the presence of uncertainty. He asserted that the mere presence of uncertainty transforms society into an "enterprise organization" that is characterized by specialization of functions. The function of the entrepreneur becomes paramount in this kind of organization as a specialized agent who reduces uncertainty (Knight 1921, p. 271).

This Knightian uncertainty is not easily compartmentalized, for it pervades all human decision-making. But it helps establish a boundary between management and entrepreneurship. According to Knight (1921, p. 276), the function of manager does not in itself imply entrepreneurship, but a manager becomes an entrepreneur when his performance requires that he exercise judgment involving liability to error. Moreover, the assumption of responsibility for the correctness of his actions is a prerequisite to getting the other members of the firm to submit to an entrepreneur's direction.

An interesting corollary of Knight's theory is that profit could not exist without error. Entrepreneurial profit depends on whether an entrepreneur can make productive services yield more than the price fixed upon them by what other people think they can make them yield. Therefore, its magnitude is based on a margin of error in calculation by entrepreneurs (and non-entrepreneurs) who do not force the successful entrepreneurs to pay as much for productive services as they could be forced to pay. It is this margin of error in judgment that constitutes the only true uncertainty in the workings of the competitive organization. Furthermore, in Knight's view it is this uncertainty that is borne by the true entrepreneur and explains profit.

Knight took the same position as Cantillon regarding the separation of capitalist and entrepreneur. Both agreed that the entrepreneur may or may not be a capitalist – usually he must of necessity own some property, just as all property owners can hardly be freed from risk and responsibility. The point both writers stressed is that whether or not an entrepreneur owns capital, the essence of entrepreneurship is not to be found therein. As Knight emphasized (1921, p. 310), "The only 'risk' which leads to [entrepreneurial] profit is a unique uncertainty resulting from an exercise of ultimate responsibility which in its very nature cannot be insured nor capitalized nor salaried."

The range of possible activities undertaken by Knight's entrepreneur are wide indeed. Taking inspiration from Knight, Donald A. Schön (1963, p. 84) portrays the entrepreneur as a champion of new ideas and technologies, accepting the risk of failure but willing to "put himself on the line for an idea of doubtful success." Schön (1976, p. 118) sees the entrepreneur as a kind of "broker" of new technologies, noting that "technological innovation requires leaps that cannot be justified before the fact by those charged with the task. So, there comes into being a man who takes the burden of risk on his shoulders without formal justification ... entrepreneurs without authority."

Jay W. Forrester (1965), however, cautions that today's entrepreneur gets but one chance to succeed – a dubious assertion, but one seconded by Modesto A. Maidique (1980). Not all economists have found Knight's formulation appropriate. Fritz Redlich (1957) contends that Knight's theory is of no use to the historian of entrepreneurship because it offers no distinction between ownership and control, on the one hand, and management and decision making, on the other.

Postscript

American economists took up the notion of the entrepreneur with increasing intensity as the nineteenth century drew to a close. The gulf between capitalist and entrepreneur was widened by the Americans during this period. Despite some disparity in perceptions and theories among American economists, the idea that the entrepreneur is not a risk-bearer began to assert itself. This represents a break with the tradition begun by Cantillon. Frank Knight steered the discussion back towards Cantillon but added the important distinction between risk and uncertainty.

7 Joseph Schumpeter

The writers surveyed up to this point worked mainly within the equilibrium tradition of mainstream economics. The Austrians and Knight were exceptions, because they were particularly interested in disequilibrium processes. In the main, however, neoclassical economics concentrated on end-states (i.e., solutions in which the effects of uncertainty have been expunged from consideration). Uncertainty in the sense of the incalculable has no meaning in this mainstream approach, because solutions to economic problems require that the actual and the calculable coincide. Deviations of one from the other, such as true uncertainty allows, cannot be fully accommodated within the equilibrium tradition. Thus Maurice Dobb (1937, p. 559) correctly asserted that "In a system of economic equilibrium the work of the entrepreneur cannot be qualitatively different from that of any other agent of production."

A more robust functional theory of entrepreneurship must allow some potential for the entrepreneur to engage in decision-making that alters the equilibrium position of the enterprise. J. B. Clark took tentative steps in this direction, but he did not complete the process. Both Clark and Joseph Schumpeter were influenced to some extent by the German historical school, a group of writers who were critical of received economic doctrine, especially the English variant. Schumpeter, as we shall see, made the innovative entrepreneur an endogenous variable and placed him at the vortex of his theory of economic development. Almost all modern theories of entrepreneurship take their origin from Schumpeter.

The German historical school

The development of economic thought in the late nineteenth and early twentieth centuries progressed differently in Germany than it did in England or the rest of the continent. This was due in part to the influence on economic method of the German historical school. The historicists believed that in order to understand man's economic behavior and the institutions that constrain it, economics must describe human motives and behavioral tendencies in psychologically realistic terms. This group of writers specifically rejected the individualistic underpinnings of English political economy and the notion that man is a "hedonistic atom" (cf. Spengler and Allen 1960, pp. 500–24).

The founders of the German historical school were Wilhelm Roscher (1817–94), Karl Knies (1821–98), and Bruno Hildebrand (1812–78). It was their contention that a thorough analysis and complete understanding of historical data were prerequisites to a proper development of economic theory. Roscher showed an early interest in the concept of the entrepreneur by expounding Turgot's version of the theory. His *Grundlagen der Nationalöekonomie*, originally published in 1854, avoided altogether the term profit, representing the entrepreneur as a managerial laborer who owns and directs a business on his own responsibility. His income, besides interest and rent, is described by Roscher as basically a wage.

The second generation of historicists is represented best by Gustav Schmoller (1838–1917). Schmoller rejected David Ricardo's abstract deductive reasoning in favor of a broad historical and empirical approach to economic theory. Consequently, he amassed mountains of historical data in order to analyze actual economic behavior. From his examination of these data, he discovered a unique central factor in all economic activity – the enterprising spirit, the *unternehmer*, or entrepreneur. Schmoller's entrepreneur was a creative organizer and manager whose role was innovation and the initiation of new projects (Zrinyi 1962). This creative organizer combined factors of production to yield either new products or new methods of production. Schmoller's entrepreneur possessed imagination and daring. He was a more distinctive force than Roscher's "superior laborer."

Schmoller's ideas were extended by third-generation historicists Werner Sombart (1863–1941) and Max Weber (1864–1920). Sombart introduced a "new leader" who animates the entire economic system by creative innovations. This entrepreneur combined the powers of organization described by Schmoller with the personality and talent to elicit maximum productivity from individuals engaged in the productive process. Whether he is a financier, manufacturer, or trader, Sombart painted the entrepreneur as a profit maximizer.

The German historicists characterized the entrepreneurial process as breaking away from the old methods of production and creating new ones. This disequilibrating process was particularly emphasized by Weber. He sought to explain how a social system, as compared to an individual enterprise, could evolve from one stable form (perhaps under an authoritarian structure) to another type of system. Historically, Weber identified such changes with a charismatic leader or entrepreneur-like person (cf. Carlin 1956).

Weber (1930, p. 67) began his analysis of change with a stationary state construct that visualizes "an economic process which merely reproduces itself at constant rates; a given population, not changing in either numbers or age distribution." In this stationary state the wants of households are given and do not change; the means of production are optimal from the standpoint of the firm's interest and likewise do not change, "unless some datum changes or some chance event intrudes upon this world."

In such a stationary society there is nothing that requires the activity traditionally associated with the entrepreneur. "No other than ordinary routine work has to be done in this stationary society," declared Weber (1930, p. 67), "either by workmen or managers." Yet, inevitably, change occurs. One likely example occurred in pre-industrial revolution Europe:

> Some young men from one of the putting-out families went out into the country, carefully chose weavers from his employ, greatly increased the rigor of his supervision of their work, and thus turned them from peasants into laborers ... he would begin to change his marketing methods ... he began to introduce the principle of low prices and large turnover. There was repeated what everywhere and always is the result of such a process of rationalization: those who would not follow suit had to go out of business. The idyllic state collapsed under the pressure of a bitter competitive struggle.
>
> (Weber 1930, p. 68)

Here we have an entrepreneur at work, upsetting the reigning equilibrium and provoking the "bitter competitive struggle" alluded to in the passage above. The critical characteristics of Weber's successful entrepreneur are his religious imperatives, which make up what is called the Protestant ethic. This reliance on religious imperatives makes Weber's theory unique and challenging, but in a way that blurs distinctions between sociology and economics. Perhaps for this reason, Weber (like Marx, and for the same reasons) remains on the periphery of mainstream economics.

The Schumpeterian perspective

Max Weber was a major influence on Joseph A. Schumpeter (1883–1950), who defended an instrumentalist methodology that treats theories as meaningful only to the extent that they yield useful results. For Schumpeter the main instrument of change in a theory of economic development is the entrepreneur. Development is a dynamic process, a disturbing of the economic status quo. Schumpeter regarded economic development not as a mere adjunct to the central body of orthodox economic theory, but as the basis for reinterpreting a vital process that had been crowded out of mainstream economic analysis by the static general equilibrium approach. The entrepreneur is a key figure for Schumpeter because, quite simply, he is the *persona causa* of economic development.

Schumpeter combined ideas from Marx, Weber, and Walras, along with insights from his Austrian forebears, Menger, von Wieser, and his teacher, von Böhm-Bawerk. Rather than slavishly imitate the work of others, he melded these elements into something uniquely his own. He shared Marx's views that economic processes are organic and that change comes from within the economic system, not merely from without (also Clark's view). He also admired the blend of sociology and economics that characterized the works of Marx and Weber. From Walras he borrowed the notion of the entrepreneur, but in place of the phantom-like figure of Walras's general equilibrium system, Schumpeter substituted a living, breathing entrepreneur of flesh and spirit. Reflecting the Austrian economists' interest in disequilibrium processes, Schumpeter made the entrepreneur the mechanism of economic change.

Entrepreneurs and innovation

To Schumpeter, competition involved mainly the dynamic innovations of the entrepreneur. This view is most clearly and completely set forth in his *Theory of Economic Development* (1912) and echoed in later works of 1939 and 1950. Although the nature of competition may change over time, the essential and pivotal role of the entrepreneur does not.[1] Schumpeter used the concept of equilibrium as Weber used the stationary state – a theoretical construct, a point of departure. He coined a phrase to describe this equilibrium state, calling it "the circular flow of economic life." Its chief characteristic is that economic life proceeds routinely on the basis of past experience; there are no forces evident for any change of the status quo. In this circular flow, only products that were produced in the previous period are consumed in each period, and only products that will be consumed in the following period are produced.

> Therefore workers and landlords always exchange their productive services for present consumption goods only, whether the former are employed directly or only indirectly in the production of consumption goods. There is no necessity for them to exchange their services of labor and land for future goods or for promises of future consumption goods or to apply for any "advances" of present consumption goods. It is simply a matter of exchange, and not of credit transactions. The element of time plays no part. All products are only products and nothing more. For the individual firm it is a matter of complete indifference whether

it produces means of production or consumption goods. In both cases the product is paid for immediately and at its full value.

(Schumpeter 1934 [1912], pp. 42–3)

In this system the production function is invariant, although factor substitution is possible within the limits of known technological horizons. The only real function that must be performed in this state is "that of combining the two original factors of production, and this function is performed in every period mechanically as it were, of its own accord, without requiring a personal element distinguishable from superintendence and similar things" (Schumpeter 1934 [1912], p. 45). In this artificial situation, the entrepreneur is a nonentity. "If we choose to call the manager or owner of a business 'entrepreneur,'" wrote Schumpeter (1934 [1912], pp. 45–6), then he would be an entrepreneur of the kind described by Walras, "without special function and without income of a special kind."

But the circular flow is a mere foil. The relevant problem, Schumpeter wrote in *Capitalism, Socialism and Democracy* (1950, p. 84), is not how capitalism administers existing structures, but how it creates and destroys them. This process – what Schumpeter called "creative destruction" – is the essence of economic development. In other words, development is a disturbance of the circular flow. It occurs in industrial and commercial life, not in consumption. It is a process defined by the carrying out of new combinations in production. And it is accomplished by the entrepreneur.

Schumpeter reduced his theory to three elemental and corresponding pairs of opposites: (1) the circular flow (i.e., tendency toward equilibrium) versus a change in economic routine or data, (2) statics versus dynamics, and (3) entrepreneurship versus management. The first pair consists of two real processes; the second, two theoretical apparatuses; the third, two distinct types of conduct. The theory maintained that the essential function of the entrepreneur is distinct from that of capitalist, landowner, laborer, and inventor. According to Schumpeter, the entrepreneur may be any and all of these things, but if he is, it is by coincidence rather than by function. Nor is the entrepreneurial function, in principle, connected with the possession of wealth, even though "the accidental fact of the possession of wealth constitutes a practical advantage" (Schumpeter 1934 [1912], p. 101). Moreover, entrepreneurs do not form a social class, in the technical sense, although they come to be esteemed for their ability in a capitalist society.

Schumpeter admitted that the essential function of the entrepreneur is almost always mingled with other functions, hence the appeal of Marshall's definition of the entrepreneur as manager. But management, he asserted, does not elicit the truly distinctive function of the entrepreneur. "The function of superintendence in itself, constitutes no essential economic distinction," he declared (1934 [1912], p. 20). The function of making decisions is another matter, however. In Schumpeter's theory, the dynamic entrepreneur is the person who innovates, who makes 'new combinations' in production.

Schumpeter described innovation in several ways. Initially he spelled out the kinds of new combinations that underlie economic development. They encompass the following: (1) creation of a new good or new quality of good, (2) creation of a new method of production, (3) the opening of a new market, (4) the capture of a new source of supply, and (5) a new organization of industry (e.g., creation or destruction of a monopoly). Over time, of course, the force of these new combinations dissipates as the "new" becomes part of the "old" (circular flow). But this does not change the essence of the entrepreneurial function. According to Schumpeter (1934 [1912], p. 78), "everyone is an entrepreneur only when he actually 'carries out new combinations,' and loses that character as soon as he has built up his business, when he settles down to running it as other people run their businesses."

Technically, Schumpeter defined innovation with reference to the production function. The production function, he said, "describes the way in which quantity of product varies if quantities of factors vary. If, instead of quantities of factors, we vary the form of the function, we have an innovation" (Schumpeter 1939, p. 62). Mere cost-reducing adaptations of knowledge lead only to new supply schedules of existing goods, however, so this kind of innovation must involve a new commodity or one of higher quality. However, Schumpeter recognized that the knowledge that kindles an innovation need not be new. On the contrary, it may be existing knowledge that has not been utilized before. There is probably no time at which the existing store of scientific knowledge can be completely exploited, but according to Schumpeter (1928, p. 378):

> It is not the knowledge that matters, but the successful solution of the task *sui generis* of putting an untried method into practice – there may be, and often is, no scientific novelty involved at all, and even if it be involved, this does not make any difference to the nature of the process.

In Schumpeter's theory, successful innovation requires an act of will, not of intellect. It depends, therefore, on leadership, not intelligence, and it should not be confused with invention. Schumpeter (1934 [1912], pp. 88–9) was insistent that innovation and invention require:

> entirely different kinds of aptitudes. Although entrepreneurs of course may be inventors just as they may be capitalists, they are inventors not

by nature of their function but by coincidence, and vice versa. Besides, the innovations that entrepreneurs carry out need not necessarily be any inventions at all."[2]

The leadership that constitutes innovation in the Schumpeterian system is not homogeneous. An aptitude for leadership stems in part from the use of knowledge, and knowledge has aspects of a public good. People of action who perceive and react to knowledge do so in various ways; each internalizes the public good in potentially a different way. The leader distances himself from the manager by virtue of his aptitude. According to Schumpeter (1928, p. 380), different aptitudes for the routine work of "static" management result merely in differential success at what all managers do, whereas different leadership aptitudes mean that "some are able to undertake uncertainties incident to what has not been done before; [indeed] … to overcome these difficulties incident to change of practice is the function of the entrepreneur."[3]

Entrepreneurial profits

Schumpeter's entrepreneurial function contrasts sharply with the managerial function described by Mill, but it has a modest affinity with Marshall's entrepreneur, who is also a leader and a person of creative imagination. Like Marshall, Schumpeter separated the entrepreneur's profits from the earnings of management. However, he flatly rejected the idea of profit as a differential rent, insisting that it not be confused with other factor returns. He argued that the "jumbling together of interest and profit" has historically caused much mischief in economics, leading many writers to the erroneous conclusion that profits are always tending "towards equalization … which does not exist at all in reality" (Schumpeter 1934 [1912], p. 153).

Like Clark, whose theory of profits he judged nearest his own, Schumpeter argued that the very existence of entrepreneurial profits means that equilibrium has been disturbed. Although entrepreneurs and profits disappear in "the circular flow of economic life," Schumpeter conceived economic reality as a dynamic process of churning from one equilibrium to the next. The real action (e.g., economic development) occurs in disequilibrium. Thus we have his claim that "Without development there is no profit, without profit no development" (Schumpeter 1934 [1912], p. 154).

But what is the fundamental nature of profit? For Schumpeter, entrepreneurial profit is a residual, a surplus of revenue over costs. A surplus may arise either because an entrepreneur's new combination of existing resources lowers costs or because it raises values (e.g., through production of new products). Either way, the size of the surplus is related to the entrepreneur's productivity, but not in the same way as the returns to the other factors of production.

The paradox of profits in the Schumpeterian system is that they are simultaneously like and unlike other factor returns. Although the analogy is tempting, Schumpeter (1934 [1912], p. 153) refused to identify profit with wages. Elaborating further, he added:

> It is certainly not a simple residuum; it is the expression of the value of what the entrepreneur contributes to production in exactly the same sense that wages are the value expression of what the worker 'produces' ... However, while wages are determined according to the marginal productivity of labor, profit is a striking exception to this law: the problem of profit lies precisely in the fact that the laws of cost and of marginal productivity seem to exclude it. And what the 'marginal entre-preneur' receives is wholly a matter of indifference for the success of the others. Every rise in wages is diffused over all wages; one who has success as an entrepreneur has it alone at first. Wages are an element in price, profit is not in the same sense. The payment of wages is one of the brakes to production, profit is not. One might say of the latter, but with more right, what the classical economists asserted of rent of land, namely that it does not enter into the price of the products.

Many earlier writers – from Cantillon to Hawley – had emphasized the connection between the entrepreneur's profit and risk. Schumpeter rejected this view. Risk falls on the capitalist, he argued, or on the owner of goods, not on the entrepreneur *qua* entrepreneur. Despite having unusual will and energy, Schumpeter's entrepreneur is a person with no capital. On this issue, Schumpeter sided with Clark and departed from his mentor, von Böhm-Bawerk, for whom the entrepreneur was clearly the capitalist, with no possibility of separation.

Schumpeter's profit theory has been roundly criticized by S. M. Kanbur (1980) for ignoring other forms of risk besides mere financial risk. Kanbur cites opportunity costs as an ingredient of entrepreneurial risk, especially for the entrepreneur who is not a capitalist. One kind of opportunity cost is the risk to reputation, of which Schumpeter (1934 [1912], p. 137) said: "Even though he [the entrepreneur] may risk his reputation, the direct responsibility of failure never falls on him." Kanbur vigorously rejects this proposition. He claims that the individual need not run an enterprise himself. Every entrepreneur may confront uncertainty in the form of self-doubt as to his entrepreneurial ability. Such uncertainty can be circumvented by taking up employment in which one is less uncertain of one's ability and lending one's capital to someone who offers better returns. To do otherwise is to risk one's reputation, as well as one's capital, at least in relation to the safe alternative. Thus Kanbur (1980, p. 493) concludes:

> The two risks can indeed be separated out for conceptual or analytical purposes, not least because the opportunity cost of the capital will, in general, be different from the opportunity cost of entrepreneurial effort, and it is relative to these opportunity costs that gains and losses, and hence risks, have to be conceptualized.

Kanbur (1979) finds the Cantillon-Knight formulation of entrepreneurship more amenable to the task of modeling entrepreneurial behavior, especially for the purpose of discovering the relationship between risk-taking and the distribution of personal income.

Having departed the scene, Schumpeter is unable to answer modern critics. But many years ago he defended his conception as non-idiosyncratic and historically legitimate:

> As it is the carrying out of new combinations that constitutes the entrepreneur, it is not necessary that he should be permanently connected with an individual firm; ... our concept is narrower than the traditional one in that it does not include all heads of firms or managers or industrialists who may operate an established business. ... Nevertheless I maintain that ... [my] definition does no more than formulate with greater precision what the traditional doctrine really means to convey. In the first place our definition agrees with the usual one on the fundamental point of distinguishing between 'entrepreneurs' and 'capitalists' – irrespective of whether the latter are regarded as owners of money, claims to money, or material goods. ... It also settles the question whether the ordinary shareholder as such is an entrepreneur, and disposes of the conception of the entrepreneur as risk bearer.
>
> (Schumpeter 1934 [1912], p. 75)

Schumpeter's defense notwithstanding, other economists have chided him for his relative neglect of the topic of uncertainty in the theory of entrepreneurship. Andreas Papandreou argued decades ago that uncertainty is fundamental to the understanding and appreciation of the environment in which entrepreneurs break away from the routine. To compensate for the deficiency in Schumpeter's theory, Papandreou (1943, p. 23) posited an alternative definition that makes uncertainty more explicit: "The entrepreneur would be the one who carries out innovation under conditions of uncertainty and unpredictability."

Postscript

Schumpeter's influence on the theory of economic development has been enormous, even among those economists who reject his theory of entrepreneurship outright. Those who would modify the theory are forced to deal with it on its original terms. Over the long haul, Schumpeter's vision and theoretical apparatus have proven more winsome to economists than Weber's. In part, this is undoubtedly because Schumpeter's theory does not depend on extra-economic factors. Both thinkers advanced leadership theories of the entrepreneur. Whereas Weber conceived the innovator as an "ideal type" of the Protestant worldly ascetic, Schumpeter portrayed him as the supernormal economic agent. The latter is a more plausible analytic stratagem, because in a theory of economic evolution it is more meaningful to postulate the appearance of someone of extraordinary economic ability as a mechanism of change than to postulate the random appearance of a John Calvin or a similar charismatic figure.

Ronan Macdonald (1971) has argued perceptively that insofar as theories of economic change go, Schumpeter's analysis occupies the middle ground between Marshall and Weber. Marshall's theory adapted incrementally to shifts in preference and production functions, the result being a continuous improvement in moral qualities, tastes, and economic techniques. Its shortcoming was that it did not explain business cycles, a deficiency that Marshall's student Keynes set about to remedy. Marshall's approach also implied a theory of linear progress, which Schumpeter's theory denies. Weber's theory developed its own set of moral imperatives and used them to explain rapid social and economic transitions that punctuate long periods of historical continuity. Schumpeter postulated the continuous occurrence of innovations and waves of adaptation, simply because entrepreneurs are always present and are a persistent force for change.

Ultimately, the appeal of Schumpeter's theory of economic development derives from its simplicity and its power. This simplicity and power are summed up in this Schumpeterian phrase: "The carrying out of new combinations we call 'enterprise'; the individual whose function it is to carry them out we call 'entrepreneurs'" (Schumpeter 1934 [1912], p. 74). Yet despite the importance of Schumpeter's contribution to economic development, the larger dynamics of his theory have failed to penetrate deeply into conventional economic analysis. However, economic historians have been more ready to apply the Schumpeterian paradigm.[4] On the pragmatic side, Albert Hirschman has tried to bolster Schumpeter's perspective by emphasizing a "cooperative" component of entrepreneurship in addition to the creative component. For Hirschman (1958, p. 17), an entrepreneur must be more than a creative "rebel." He must also embody "the ability to engineer agreement among all interested parties, such as the inventor of the [new] process, the partner, the capitalist, the supplier of parts and services, the distributors, etc." Like many theories developed in the aftermath of Schumpeter's performance, however, this added perspective is a complement to, rather than a substitute for, the basic theory.

8   Beyond Schumpeter

Schumpeter's theory of economic development and the theory of entrepreneurship within it stimulated a new wave of research on entrepreneurship in the twentieth century. Reaction by twentieth-century writers has been quite diverse, however. At Harvard University, Schumpeter's academic base of operations in the United States, a tradition began that studied the entrepreneur from the standpoint of economic history. Other writers have been more concerned with the analytics of Schumpeter's theory, especially the question of whether the entrepreneur is an equilibrating or disequilibrating force. Still other writers divide themselves along neoclassical and Austrian lines. In this chapter we expose and examine these different approaches and the writers who advanced them.

Harvard historical studies

In the wake of Schumpeter's treatment of economic development, a tradition of historical studies of entrepreneurship began at Harvard University's Research Center in Entrepreneurial History, established by Arthur H. Cole (1889–1974). Cole's interest in the entrepreneur and his views on the subject were influenced by Edwin F. Gay (1867–1946), founder of the Economic History Association and a follower of Schumpeter. The entrepreneur as a disequilibrating agent of change occupies a prominent place in Gay's philosophy of history, which asserts that the amount of permissible free competition existing in society varies with social need. In this system of free competition the entrepreneur is a self-centered actor and a disruptive force, but according to Gay (1923–24, p. 12), "There are periods in the rhythm of history when ... that disruptive, innovating energy is socially advantageous and must be given freer opportunity."

Following Gay's lead, Cole decried the neglect of the entrepreneur by economic historians and economic theorists. In order to discover the uniqueness of entrepreneurship and its importance to economics, Cole advocated a case-study approach that employed various methods, including cross-sectional investigations of specific individuals over time, longitudinal studies of particular entrepreneurial functions (e.g., trends in personnel policies), and conceptual studies in historical entrepreneurship capable of providing solutions to current problems.[1]

Cole's entrepreneur possesses two noteworthy features, each of which has early antecedents in economics. First, he is a productive agent who utilizes other productive factors for the creation of goods. Second, he makes decisions under uncertainty. In what was the most comprehensive (if not the most wordy) definition of entrepreneurship since von Wieser, Cole (1949, p. 88) defined entrepreneurship as:

> the purposeful activity (including an integrated sequence of decisions) of an individual or group of associated individuals, undertaken to initiate, maintain, or aggrandize a profit-oriented business unit for the production or distribution of economic goods and services with pecuniary or other advantage the goal or measure of success, in interaction with (or within the conditions established by) the internal situation of the unit itself or with the economic, political, and social circumstances (institutions and practices) of a period which allows an appreciable measure of freedom of decision.

"Purposeful activity" is potentially a multifarious concept. We take it to mean that entrepreneurial activity is directed toward some goal, presumably profit maximization. However, it may also refer to the rational ability to make decisions and to implement them.[2] "An integrated sequence of decisions" suggests the importance of organization in the conceptual understanding of entrepreneurship, a theme amplified by Leland H. Jenks (1949).[3] The "business unit" as an institutional datum therefore constitutes the basis for a theory of entrepreneurial action in this view. Jenks (1949, p. 151) asserted that "Business unit and entrepreneur are interdependent conceptions. A business unit consists of a system of entrepreneurial and non-entrepreneurial roles structured as a system of exchange sets, productive performers, and cooperative activities."

This passage illustrates a major theme of the Harvard economic historians, namely that the definition and meaning of entrepreneurship must be associated with environmental characteristics that influence the entrepreneur's decision-making process. In this Cole and the others have followed Schumpeter's lead, since he perceived that the innovative actions of the entrepreneur impact upon the environment in symbiotic fashion.

Shackle's anti-equilibrium approach

Across the Atlantic, G. L. S. Shackle (1903–1992) expressed his belief that entrepreneurs *make* history. Shackle focused his attention on the psychic act of decision in the world of enterprise. At an early point in his investigation of the nature and essence of business enterprise, Shackle (1955) identified two roles that must be performed. One is bearing uncertainty; the other is making decisions. These two roles are not unrelated, because decision-making involves improvisation or invention – actions that are genuinely possible only in a world of unknowns and uncertainties.

Shackle was at his best in explicating the nature of business decisions and the scope for human action within them. An astute Marshallian, he was critical of mainstream economic theory's failure to recognize Marshall's primary discovery – the role of time in the world of affairs. Time, Shackle said, weaves an historical tapestry, the threads of which are the consequences of human decisions. Thus:

> We take it for granted that a responsibility lies upon us for our acts; that these acts are in a profound sense creative, inceptive, the source of historical novelty; that each such act is, as it were, the unconnected starting point of a new thread in the tapestry which time is weaving.
>
> (Shackle 1966, p. 73)

Time and uncertainty are close kin. Shackle's approach to entrepreneurship faces uncertainty squarely and rejects deterministic models, but it affirms that some sort of order holds in the world of practical affairs. In sum, his research agenda calls for the reconciliation of uncertainty and imaginative experience, two elements that comprise every business decision. But what is uncertainty? To Shackle, uncertainty is a state of mind, something subjective. This subjective magnitude is nevertheless bounded by possibility, a condition required to keep the problem under investigation within the scope of analytic manipulation. Shackle (1966, p. 86) maintains that without bounds to human action, an individual is powerless to affect the course of events; hence, "It is only a bounded uncertainty that will permit him to act creatively."

According to Shackle, business decisions involve imagination and choice in the face of bounded uncertainty. Most of Shackle's work elaborates the second of these two elements. Eschewing the ambiguous term "entrepreneur," Shackle calls decision-makers "enterprisers." He reserves this term for those engaged in production who actually bear uncertainty, recognizing that "those who wish can contract out of uncertainty" (Shackle 1955, p. 82). Whereas making decisions and bearing uncertainty could be considered two roles instead of one, for Shackle the enterpriser is the single individual who takes on both roles.

Although the motive behind this shift in terminology is plain, there is nevertheless strong kinship between Shackle's enterpriser and Cantillon's entrepreneur. Shackle attempts to get inside the entrepreneur's head, as it were, in order to discover the basis of enterprising decisions. In the process, he reflects a combination of Marshallian, Keynesian, and Austrian concerns. Like Marshall, he seeks to integrate fully the effects of time into the economics of decision-making. Like Keynes, he confronts the matter of uncertainty of business decisions. Like Menger, *et al.*, he is a radical subjectivist. Yet there are important differences, too. Unlike either of the above, Shackle's approach to economics is psychological and anti-equilibrium.

Shackle regarded his own work as an extension of a Keynesian problem, namely the determinants of business investment. He perceived a fundamental inconsistency in the Keynesian paradigm. He called Keynes's *General Theory* "a paradox, for its central concern is with uncertainty, decisions based on conjecture, and situations altogether lacking in objective stability, yet it uses an equilibrium method" (Shackle 1955, p. 222). In reaction to this anomaly, Shackle jettisoned the equilibrium method – a radical stroke that probably accounts for the failure of mainstream economics to take him more seriously. Shackle's true followers are relatively few. The most prominent is Ludwig Lachmann, who also exhibits strong Austrian tendencies.

Entrepreneurship and human capital

Nobel laureate T.W. Schultz (1902–1998) has advanced a theory of entrepreneurship fully within the neoclassical paradigm. Schultz finds in contemporary economic literature a persistent failure to see the rewards that accrue to those who bring about economic equilibration, especially as it occurs in certain non-market activities. A leading pioneer of human capital theory, Schultz approached entrepreneurship from this angle. He criticized the standard concept and treatment of entrepreneurship mainly on four grounds: (1) the concept is usually restricted to businessmen, (2) it does not take into account the differences in allocative abilities among entrepreneurs, (3) the supply of entrepreneurship is not treated as a scarce resource, and (4) entrepreneurship is neglected whenever general equilibrium considerations dominate economic inquiry (Schultz 1975, p. 832).

Schultz made two major advances. First, he redefined the concept of entrepreneurship as "the ability to deal with disequilibria" and extended the notion to non-market activities (e.g., household decisions, allocation of time) as well as market activities. Second, he provided evidence of the effects of education on people's ability to perceive and react to disequilibria. He argued that Schumpeter did not go far enough in his formulation. "Whether or not economic growth is deemed to be 'progress,'" declared Schultz (1975, p. 832), "it is a process beset with various classes of disequilibria." To be sure Schumpeter's entrepreneur "creates developmental disequilibria," but Schumpeter did not extend the entrepreneur's function successfully to "all manner of other disequilibria," including laborers who are reallocating their labor services or students, housewives, and consumers who are reallocating their resources, mainly time.

Schultz (1980, p. 438) also contended that Schumpeter's entrepreneurs have become a decreasing part of the technological story in present-day society because of the growth of research and development in the public sector, a development that Schumpeter could not have anticipated. In point of fact, Schumpeter spent many pages in his *Capitalism, Socialism and Democracy* (3rd edition, 1950) explicitly lamenting the fact that the growth of bureaucracy dampens the pioneering and innovating spirit.

Unlike Shackle, Schultz has vigorously defended the equilibrium method. He claimed that "Unless we develop equilibrating models, the function of this particular ability [entrepreneurship] cannot be analyzed" (Schultz 1975, p. 843). Therefore Schultz widened the concept of entrepreneurship so that it embraced *any* economic agent that has the ability to deal with disequilibria; and he insisted that the supply of entrepreneurial ability is a scarce economic resource.

The supply of entrepreneurial ability is a sticking point for some economists. Schultz's theory attempted to discriminate between the disequilibria faced by firms, households, and individuals in order to trace out supply functions for the useful ability to deal with disequilibria. Supply, in this sense, "depends upon the stock of a particular form of human capital at any point in time and on the costs and the rate at which the stock can be increased in response to the rewards derived from the services of these abilities" (Schultz 1975, p. 834). Testing the effects of education in this connection, Schultz found it to be a strong explanatory variable.[4]

At base, Schultz's approach to entrepreneurship was shaped by his firm commitment to the neoclassical paradigm. According to this paradigm, because entrepreneurial ability is a useful service, entrepreneurs must have an identifiable marginal product. Accordingly, there must be a "market" for the service in the sense of normal supply and demand functions. Schultz summarized his argument in the following manner, in which he resurrected the von Mangoldt–Marshall position that the value of entrepreneurial activity is a differential return to ability.

The substance of my argument is that disequilibria are inevitable in [a] dynamic economy. These disequilibria cannot be eliminated by law, by public policy, and surely not by rhetoric. A modern dynamic economy would fall apart were it not for the entrepreneurial actions of a wide array of human agents who reallocate their resources and thereby bring their part of the economy back into equilibrium. Every entrepreneurial decision to reallocate resources entails risk. What entrepreneurs do has an economic value. This value accrues to them as a rent, i.e., a rent which is a reward for their entrepreneurial performance. This reward is *earned.* Although this reward for the entrepreneurship of most human agents is small, in the aggregate in a dynamic economy it accounts for a substantial part of the increases in national income. The concealment of this part in the growth of national income implies that entrepreneurs have not received their due in economics.

(Schultz 1980, p. 443)

According to Schultz (1975, p. 843), explicitly recognizing the connection between entrepreneurship and education is merely "the first step on what appears to be a long new road." This new road is sure to contain many potholes and detours. At the most basic level, for example, it is not clear what the precise connection is between education and knowledge. Fritz Machlup (1902–1983), reflecting the influence of Friedrich Hayek, argued that formal education is only one form of knowledge; knowledge is also gained experientially and at different rates by different individuals. Individuals can accrue knowledge from their day-to-day experiences, claimed Machlup (1980, p. 179) which "will normally induce reflection, interpretations, discoveries, and generalizations." Moreover, the cost of acquiring knowledge is related to differential abilities.

Some alert and quick-minded persons, by keeping their eyes and ears open for new facts and theories, discoveries and opportunities, perceive what normal people of lesser alertness and perceptiveness, would fail to notice. Hence new knowledge is available at little or no cost to those who are on the lookout, full of curiosity, and bright enough not to miss their chances.

(Machlup 1980, p. 179)

Should we, therefore, synthesize Schultz and Machlup to construe that entrepreneurial abilities stem from cognitive and experiential events? Investments in factual knowledge are clearly possible, but there may yet remain innate differences in individual capacities to receive and assimilate knowledge from surroundings. If so, the human capital approach to entrepreneurship may ultimately rest on a genetic base.

A noteworthy feature of the human capital approach is that it rejects the idea of entrepreneurial rewards as a return to risk. Schultz maintained that although risk is omnipresent in a dynamic economy, there is no exclusive connection between risk and entrepreneurial activity. In his words, "the bearing of risk is not a unique attribute of entrepreneurs. Whereas entrepreneurs assume risk, there also are people who are not entrepreneurs who assume risk" (Schultz 1980, p. 441). Thus the tension between risk and uncertainty continued to mount in the economics literature well into the twentieth century.

The Austrian revival

Before the dark shadow of Hitler's Third Reich crept over the entire continent, a number of second-generation Austrian economists emigrated from Europe in the 1930s. Friedrich Hayek (1889–1992) went to London. Ludwig von Mises (1881–1973) and Joseph Schumpeter, both students of von Böhm-Bawerk, came to America. Although Schumpeter quickly found an academic home in the United States, von Mises had a difficult time. Eventually he joined the faculty at New York University under special arrangement. There he became the standard bearer of Austrian economics, reaching out intellectually to a small but capable group of students and followers.

Von Mises defined economics as the study of human action. Obviously human action embraces a wide range of activities. Human action that is distinctly economic takes place in a market framework. According to von Mises, the nature of market activity is that it is an entrepreneurial process. Like Clark, Knight, and Schumpeter, who developed their theories by first introducing artificial constructs of the economy (i.e., the static state; the circular flow) and then hypothesizing how entrepreneurial activity alters these states, von Mises built his theory upon the notion of "the evenly rotating economy." The evenly rotating economy represents a rigid picture of the world – a state of equilibrium characterized by the absence of change in date and time. It is a world of perfect price stability where market prices and final prices coincide. In such a setting, human behavior can be nothing more than involuntary response. According to von Mises (1949, p. 249), "This system is not peopled with living men making choices and liable to error; it is a world of soulless unthinking automatons; it is not a human society, it is an ant hill." Only when human action is viewed as "purposeful behavior" will change occur, because "action is change." The express purpose of the evenly rotating economy is merely to provide a point of departure for construction of a realistic theory.[5]

A fundamental aspect of Misesian human action is that it influences the future and is influenced by the future. Von Mises (1949, p. 253) declared that "The outcome of action is always uncertain. Action is always speculation." Thus participants in the actual economy make choices and cope with the subsequent uncertainties of the future. In this context, "The term entrepreneur ... means ... acting man exclusively seen from the aspect of uncertainty inherent in every action" (von Mises 1949, p. 254). It follows that in the evenly rotating system, no one is an entrepreneur; but in the actual economy, "every actor is always an entrepreneur" (von Mises 1949, p. 253).

By this view, capitalists who lend their assets with less than perfect certainty of repayment are entrepreneurs (although this does not imply that entrepreneurs must be capitalists). So too are farmers; in fact no proprietor of any factor of production is untouched by uncertainty. Laborers are also entrepreneurs because their wages are determined by uncertain market activities. What we have here is a logical extension of Cantillon's original view of the entrepreneur. Casting a wider net, von Mises brought the landowners and laborers excluded by Cantillon into the entrepreneurial fold. In other words, von Mises generalized uncertainty to all market activity.

Like many writers before him, von Mises examined the role of the entrepreneur in the context of the theory of income distribution. He distinguished between functional distribution and historical distribution, drawing attention to the entrepreneur in each and exposing the ambiguity of the concept in its dual use. On the one hand, von Mises said, economics uses the term entrepreneur in a general sense (those who receive a functional share of aggregate income), and on the other hand it uses the term in the narrower sense of those "who are especially eager to profit from adjusting production to the expected changes in conditions, those who have more initiative, more venturesomeness, and a quicker eye than the crowd, the pushing and promoting pioneers of economic improvement." He concluded that it is awkward to use the same to signify two different notions and that it might be "more expedient to employ another term for this second notion – for instance, the term 'promoter'" (von Mises 1949, pp. 254–5).

It is tempting to identify this second type of economic agent with the Schumpeterian entrepreneur, especially inasmuch as von Mises (1949, p. 255) argued that "The driving force of the market, the element tending toward unceasing innovation and improvement, is provided by the restlessness of the promoter and his eagerness to make profits as large as possible." But von Mises took pains to distinguish his conception of the entrepreneur from Schumpeter's. Referring to "errors due to the confusion of entrepreneurial activity and technological innovation and improvement," von Mises (1951, p. 11–12) argued that "Changes in ... consumers' demand may require adjustments which have no reference at all to technological innovations and improvements." The entrepreneur's job is not merely to experiment with new technological methods, he asserted, but to select from a host of technologically feasible methods:

those which are best fit to supply the public in the cheapest way with the things they are asking for most urgently. Whether a new technological procedure is or is not fit for this purpose is to be provisionally decided by the entrepreneur and will be finally decided by the conduct of the buying public.

So although it is the function of the entrepreneur to make decisions, decisions involving innovation and technological improvements do not constitute an exhaustive set where the entrepreneur is concerned.

In the capitalist tradition of economic development, profit and loss are the carrot and stick of entrepreneurial activity. "It is the entrepreneurial decision," said von Mises (1951, p. 21), "that creates either profit or loss," not capital itself, as Marx thought. Capital can be used in support of either good or bad (mistaken) ideas. If it is utilized in support of a good idea, profit results; if it is used to underwrite a bad idea, losses occur. He added: "It is the mental acts, the mind of the entrepreneur, from which profits ultimately originate. Profit is a product of the mind, of success in anticipating the future state of the market."

However one perceives the differences between von Mises's theory of entrepreneurship and Schumpeter's, there appears to be no significant differences at all between von Mises and Knight on this issue. Von Mises, of course, brought some traditional Austrian concerns to the discussion, but on practically every fundamental point dealing with the subject of entrepreneurship he comes across as a "Knightian." His precise intellectual debt to Knight remains, however, a matter of speculation.

The most provocative of the "new" theories of entrepreneurship from the Austrian camp has been put forward by von Mises's student, Israel Kirzner (1930–). For Kirzner the essence of entrepreneurship is alertness to profit opportunities. Acknowledging the combined influence of von Mises and Hayek, Kirzner offers his theory as a halfway house between the "neoclassical" view of Schultz and the "radical" view of Shackle. He bases his approach to entrepreneurship on three important ideas. The first is von Mises's central vision of the market as an entrepreneurial process. The second is Hayek's vital insight that the marketplace engenders a learning process. And the third is the conviction that entrepreneurial activities are creative acts of discovery (Kirzner 1985, p. x).

Like Shackle, Kirzner is critical of mainstream economics because it leaves no room for purposeful human action. But unlike Shackle, Kirzner does not wish to abandon the framework of economic equilibrium. Therefore Kirzner accepts that the role of the entrepreneur is to achieve the kind of adjustment necessary to move economic markets toward the equilibrium state. This crucial role is overlooked, he contends, by economic models that focus on equilibrium results rather than on the process of equilibrium.

Following von Mises, Kirzner (1979a, p. 110) maintains that mainstream neoclassical economics – as equilibrium analysis – defines "a state in which each decision correctly anticipates all other decisions," one in which decisions are made and actions taken by mere mechanical calculations; judgment has no place; and each market participant makes decisions that merely adjust given means to suit a given end. By contrast, in the Misesian dynamic economy knowledge is neither complete nor perfect, therefore markets are constantly in states of disequilibrium, and it is disequilibrium that gives scope to the entrepreneurial function.

In his earliest formulation of entrepreneurship, Kirzner seemed to depart from von Mises in several ways, thereby drawing fire from otherwise friendly critics. One objection has been leveled against Kirzner's "pure and penniless entrepreneur," that is, an entrepreneur who does not own any capital. The gist of the criticism is that if one has nothing to lose, there is no sense in which he can be said to bear risk, which is the essence of von Mises's concept of entrepreneurship. Von Mises (1951, p. 13) wrote: "There is a simple rule of thumb to tell entrepreneurs from non-entrepreneurs. The entrepreneurs are those on whom the incidence of losses on the capital employed falls." Independently of von Mises, yet allegedly in the same tradition, Kirzner argues that the essence of entrepreneurship is alertness to perceived profit opportunities. This is an idea that is implicit in the works of von Wieser and von Mises, although they failed to develop its full implications.

In his lectures Kirzner likes to stress the analogy that the entrepreneur is a person who, upon seeing a $10 bill on the ground in front of him, is alert to the opportunity and quickly grabs it. The alert person will seize it quickly; the less alert will take longer to recognize the opportunity and to act upon it. Not all entrepreneurs are created equal. By stressing pure alertness in this fashion, Kirzner emphasizes the quality of perception, recognizing an opportunity that is a sure thing, whereas in reality every profit opportunity is uncertain. Kirzner's best-known case for illustrating alertness is that of the arbitrageur, the person who, because of differences in intertemporal or interspatial demands, discovers the opportunity to buy at low prices and sell the same items at high prices. In these cases, Kirzner's entrepreneur requires neither capital, as does von Mises's entrepreneur, nor imagination, as does Shackle's enterpriser.

In response to critics, Kirzner has elaborated his view of entrepreneurship vis-à-vis uncertainty. Lawrence White (1976) and Murray Rothbard (1985) – in his endorsement of a discussion by Robert F. Hébert (1985) – questioned the role of uncertainty in Kirzner's view of the entrepreneur. The issue raised by these writers is that arbitrage deals with present, known opportunities to exploit price differences that exceed transactions/transfer costs over time or space, whereas uncertainty exists solely with respect to the future. By confining entrepreneurial activity to the practice of arbitrage, therefore, Kirzner downplays the importance of uncertainty in human decision-making. The consequences are important to economic analysis because a theory that ignores uncertainty cannot explain entrepreneurial losses, only entrepreneurial gains.[6]

Kirzner has recently confronted this asymmetry and altered his position somewhat. He now contends that uncertainty is central to the notion of entrepreneurial activity but the relationship is more subtle than formerly supposed. Entrepreneurship that is also arbitrageurship involves discovery of past error (i.e., a single-period market decision), whereas entrepreneurship in the face of uncertainty involves multi-period market decisions requiring the imagination and creativity of Shackle's enterpriser. Both views define profit opportunities, but the latter gives wider scope to the framework-constructing talents of the entrepreneur and therefore emphasizes his history-making role. The former view, by contrast, emphasizes calculation and judgment by the entrepreneur within a given framework.

As a result, Kirzner now defends a synthetic view of entrepreneurship that combines the epoch-making activities of the entrepreneur (*à la* Shackle) with the corrective adjustments of the arbitrageur, which he formerly stressed. In this new form, the nature of entrepreneurship is more directly traced backwards through von Mises to the original formulation of Cantillon. Time and uncertainty may alter the form of action called entrepreneurship, but they do not change the entrepreneur's essential function. This realization is the basis for Kirzner's wider view that:

> In the single-period case alertness can at best discover hitherto over-looked current facts. In the multi-period case entrepreneurial alertness must include the entrepreneur's perception of the way in which creative and imaginative action may vitally shape the kind of transactions that will be entered into in future market periods.
>
> (Kirzner 1985, pp. 63–4)

In other words, one must specify the nature of the market process under investigation in order to understand the concrete manifestation of the entrepreneurial function within that process.

The notion of a normal supply curve of entrepreneurial ability became a major issue of contention between Kirzner and Schultz. Schultz (1980, p. 439) criticized Kirzner for neglecting entrepreneurship as a scarce resource (i.e., failing to treat it in terms of a supply curve). Kirzner (1985, p. 89) responded that it is simply not useful to do so, because alertness involves no identifiable costs or required amounts. There has been no rapprochement on this issue, because the two contestants have been at cross-purposes. Schultz conceives entrepreneurial ability as a service – which, if it can be narrowly defined, may be amenable to the notion of a schedule of prices and quantities.[7] However, Kirzner regards alertness (i.e., entrepreneurship) as a human characteristic that is either present or not. For Kirzner, alertness, like beauty, cannot be fundamentally augmented once nature has bestowed its individual allotments.

Despite this fundamental disagreement, the theories of Kirzner and Schultz touch on a number of important issues. Both writers view the entrepreneur as someone who perceives the opportunity for gain in a disequilibrium situation and acts accordingly. Both believe that the concept is all-important and much more extensive in scope than it has heretofore been represented in economic literature. The lines of demarcation between the two theories tend to be drawn on methodological rather than analytical grounds.

Entrepreneurship and X–inefficiency

Neo-Austrian economists such as Kirzner offer a theoretical alternative to the general equilibrium paradigm of neoclassical economics. Their framework eschews the comparative-statics, perfect-markets vision of economic activity in favor of a system that emphasizes change, error, and imperfections in markets and in human decision-making. Yet theirs is not the only challenge to the dominant paradigm, for we have seen that Clark, Schumpeter, and Shackle have all launched successful criticisms and alternative visions of the neoclassical framework. Another recent challenge that has come from outside the Austrian circle is the theory of X-efficiency devised by Harvey Leibenstein (1922–1994).

It is debatable whether entrepreneurship is central or incidental to Leibenstein's theory. What is clear is that the X-efficiency paradigm excludes precisely those aspects of the neoclassical framework that virtually eliminated the role of the entrepreneur. In a perfectly competitive world of general equilibrium, all participants are viewed as successful maximizers of utility and all firms are treated as efficient producers. Leibenstein rejects this vision, substituting inefficiency as the norm. The market imperfections that account for X-inefficiency in Leibenstein's (1979) theory arise chiefly from organizational entropy, human inertia, incomplete contracts between economic agents, and conflicting agent-principal interests. In the X-inefficient world, firms do not necessarily maximize profits, nor do they always minimize costs. Obviously, one's view of what the entrepreneur does depends on one's vision of the market. The X-inefficient world is one of persistent slack, which implies the existence of entrepreneurial opportunities. According to Leibenstein (1968), these opportunities fall into four categories: connection of different markets, correction of market deficiencies (gap filling), completion of inputs, and creation or extension of time-binding, input-transforming entities (that is, firms). But Leibenstein's entrepreneur must work hard to discover such opportunities. The existence of slack and the fact that not all inputs are marketed tend to obscure profit signals, so they must be ferreted out. A world with as many market imperfections as Leibenstein's must nevertheless give as wide a scope for entrepreneurial activity as a perfectly competitive situation takes away from it.

Leibenstein emphasizes the input-completing function as the critical role of the entrepreneur. This involves filling gaps in the production process and overcoming obstacles to production. Leibenstein (1979, p. 134) asserts that "There are both empty spaces and fuzzy areas between what is being bought, and what can be done for productive purposes with what is bought."[8] In his view, motivation is the one input that is always missing. He treats individual effort as a variable in production, and because of this, denies the existence of a unique production function. This last fact adds a dimension of entrepreneurial uncertainty that is augmented by organizational entropy within the firm, which the entrepreneur must try to overcome. According to Leibenstein (1979, p. 135):

> [P]roduct space is not continuous. It is not so dense everywhere that every variety of product exists. Products come in discontinuous chunks, as it were, and not as individual characteristics or qualities. Hence the entrepreneur has to marshal enough of the missing or difficult to get inputs to produce an integrated collection of qualities.

Leibenstein's vision leads to an open-ended theory of profits. In answer to the question of what entrepreneurs get, Leibenstein replies, "whatever they can, or are clever enough to arrange to get." The X-inefficiency framework does not favor one theory of profit over another; it emphasizes a menu of contractual possibilities. As incomplete completers, entrepreneurs are put in a strategic position to work out favorable contracts that determine the size and form of their reward. They may become residual claimants, either individually or as a member of a group of residual claimants. Alternatively they can take a fixed and immediate share of the capitalized value of the enterprise. Or they can appoint themselves manager so that they may receive both a wage and a share in the residual claims (Leibenstein 1979, p. 136).

Leibenstein's paradigm seems to intersect Austrian theory at a number of critical junctures, yet neo-Austrian theorists have remained skeptical of its analytical potency. Neo-Austrians have a tendency to interpret Leibenstein's entrepreneurship as merely one interesting feature of the economic land-scape, not as a factor central to the economic process. Kirzner (1979b, p. 142) has written that Leibenstein's entrepreneurship "is a feature that indeed seems to come into focus when observed through the X-efficiency lens; but the X-efficiency paradigm can be presented without any special reference to entrepreneurs." By contrast, neo-Austrians treat the entrepreneur as the key to understanding the entire course of economic phenomena. It is through the entrepreneur's thoughts and actions that what happens in the disequilibrium state is made intelligible.

Postscript

Schumpeter's theory of economic development and the prominence it gave to the entrepreneur sparked a host of studies at Harvard University and elsewhere that attempted to put a historical face on the entrepreneur. But throughout most of the twentieth century, theories about the nature and role of entrepreneurship have focused on one issue or the other: either the cleavage between risk and uncertainty or the issue of equilibration versus disequilibration. These issues remain mostly unresolved as we enter the twenty-first century. Nevertheless, twentieth-century writers showed a marked tendency to widen the notion of entrepreneurship to the point that almost every economic action involving uncertainty and/or adjustment to disequilibria involves some element of entrepreneurship.

9 The entrepreneur and the firm

Economic theory and tradition present us with two basic explanations of why things are produced and distributed as they are. One explanation says that the price mechanism is the allocator of resources, the integrative force in a market economy. Another says that the entrepreneur performs this function. The first economist to ask why one integrating force, the entrepreneur, should substitute for another, the price system, was Ronald Coase (1910–). In a pioneer article, "The Nature of the Firm," Coase (1937) questioned why *firms* are commonly used as resource allocation mechanisms, when economic theory dictates that the price mechanism is an efficient allocator in competitive markets. If the competitive price system is an efficient allocator of resources, why do we have firms? And given that firms exist, does their presence imply market failure, as some writers have suggested?[1]

Transaction costs and the firm

In answering these questions, Coase applied the Marshallian principle of substitution-at-the-margin to his investigation of the internal workings of organizations. He asserted that firms exist because using the price system imposes costs that can be reduced or overcome by administrative arrangements. These costs are numerous and varied, but to Coase the most significant was the cost of discovering what the relevant prices are in a market system. Contract and transaction costs for multiple exchanges make up most of the other costs he identified.[2] In Coase's view, production can be organized through the price mechanism, an impersonal means of allocating resources, or through the administrative channels of a firm guided by a person or persons we shall call the entrepreneur.

Coase's theory of the firm offers an economic explanation for vertical integration. The entrepreneur's function within the firm is to detect where the costs of transferring resources from one stage of production to another via the price system (i.e., exchange) are high relative to the costs of transferring them via administrative act. Donald Boudreaux (1986, p. 18), an economist who has studied Coase carefully, summarized:

> If an entrepreneur notices 'excessive' costs hindering the movement of resources from one stage to another, he internalizes the various stages of production so that they come under one roof of common ownership. This internalization economizes on transaction costs that would otherwise attend the transfer of resources from one stage of production to the next.

The limit to this kind of activity by the entrepreneur is determined by the costs of establishing and maintaining administrative arrangements that supplant the price mechanism. The costs of administrative direction rise with the size of the firm – that is, with the increasing number and complexity of administrative arrangements that comprise the firm's institutional network. Thus the efficient entrepreneur is always substituting at the margin. He increases the size of the firm whenever the costs of exchanging resources across lines of ownership exceed the costs of doing so by administrative action. He decreases the size of the firm whenever the costs of administrative transfer exceed the costs of market transfer. It follows that the entrepreneur's profit is equal to the cost saving achieved by changing the firm's size in line with this principle.

In this view the firm is a true and literal substitute for the price mechanism because – as in general equilibrium price theory – the entrepreneur's task is preordained. He is merely required to calculate administrative versus market costs and adjust his organization accordingly in line with the profit incentive. On close examination, the nature of decision-making in this kind of firm involves neither human discretion nor uncertainty bearing. The chief merit of this view has been the illumination of transaction costs and how they affect the nature of the firm.

A "transaction costs" approach to the firm was pioneered independently by Arnold Plant (1937), who attempted to explain why firms become centralized or decentralized. Subsequent independent inquiries into organization theory by Edith Penrose, Alfred D. Chandler, Jr., and H. B. Malmgren also extended the analysis initiated by Coase. Penrose (1959) theorized that firms evolve in a dynamic state of rivalrous competition as a consequence of the plans and willful acts of entrepreneurs. The growth and prosperity of each firm, therefore, depends on the entrepreneur's ability to plan effectively and to devise efficient administrative mechanisms and hierarchies.

Chandler (1962) advanced the thesis that a firm's administrative structure is primarily a function of its business strategy. The connection to entrepreneurship is that he regards business strategy as an entrepreneurial activity because it involves foresight, deliberation, planning and dealing with uncertainty.

Malmgren (1961) refined Coase's analysis by his thoughtful elaboration of the costs involved in using the price system to allocate resources. These costs are attributable primarily to market imperfections and uncertain input prices. Malmgren (1961, p. 399) concluded that "The market operates between firms, but the entrepreneur is the planning and coordinating agent within the bounds of any one firm." Unlike Coase, he stressed uncertainty, but he confined uncertainty only to input prices and quantities. Both Coase and Malmgren considered the final end of the production process as fixed, so the entrepreneur's judgment in either case does not extend to the choice of which product to produce.

Entrepreneurs and output-price uncertainty

This last issue affords a point of contrast between theories of the firm advanced by Coase on the one hand and Knight on the other. Like all theories that forsake uncertainty, Coase's theory focused on the execution of economic activity rather than its conception and planning. Knight emphasized conception and planning, noting how the presence of uncertainty induces major changes in the organon of economic theory. "With uncertainty present," Knight (1921, p. 268) wrote, "doing things, the actual execution of activity, becomes in a real sense a secondary part of life: the primary problem or function is deciding what to do and how to do it." Knight recognized that producers take the responsibility of forecasting consumers' wants. But he insisted that:

> [T]he work of forecasting and at the same time a large part of the technological direction and control of production are still further concentrated upon a very narrow class of the producers, and we meet with a new economic functionary, the entrepreneur.

According to Knight, this rise of the entrepreneur class brings about major changes in the basic form of business organization. Internal organization of a business cannot be entrusted to chance or to mere mechanical formula in the face of uncertainty. Entrepreneurs are required to make discretionary decisions. Firms are compelled to recognize the disparity among individuals regarding intellect, judgment, and venturesomeness. The successful business must establish an organizational structure to promote successful decision-making. It does so, according to Knight (1921, pp. 269–70), by encouraging the confident and venturesome to assume the risk that the doubtful and timid wish to avoid. In a phrase, entrepreneurs "insure" the latter group by guaranteeing them a specified income in return for a share of the enterprise's outcome.

In sum, the Knightian firm exists because the real world cannot meet all the conditions for competitive equilibrium dictated by economic theory. Knight held that the price system is effective in allocating resources among alternative uses but that it does not establish the pattern of alternative uses, which is established by entrepreneurs. Thus the essence of entrepreneurship is judgment, born of uncertainty. "Any degree of effective exercise of judgment, or making decisions," Knight (1921, p. 271) wrote, "is in a free society coupled with a corresponding degree of uncertainty-bearing, of taking the responsibility for those decisions." This responsibility is expressed in the collateral guarantees of fixed remuneration given to resource suppliers by the entrepreneur.

As we noted previously, in its basic form and content, Knight's theory of entrepreneurship is the logical extension of Cantillon's early and rich insight into how markets work. It is also a logical antecedent to Coase's theory. The opportunity for transactions to take place must exist before the cost of such transactions can be used to explain the nature of the firm. Coase's analysis takes for granted the primary question of what to produce. Insofar as it emphasizes calculation rather than judgment, it provides no meaningful way to distinguish the entrepreneur from other hired inputs. In other words, Coase worked within the confines of standard neoclassical price theory. He adopted the static, general equilibrium method of analysis, which abstracts from time and uncertainty. As a theory of the firm, his analysis is imaginative and insightful. As a theory of the entrepreneur, however, it is limited in scope and substance.

Like Coase, Knight considered it anomalous that firms exist in a regime of perfect competition. To explain the anomaly, he pushed economic analysis outside the standard neoclassical paradigm. In place of the perfect foresight hypothesized in static, general equilibrium models, he substituted entrepreneurial judgment. He made uncertainty the cornerstone of his theory, and he adopted Cantillon's concept of uncertainty (refined to distinguish between insurable and uninsurable risks). This practice places uncertainty at the point of final consumer goods and services. One can almost hear the echo of Cantillon in the following passage:

> [T]he main uncertainty which affects the entrepreneur is that connected with the sale price of his product. His position in the price system is typically that of a purchaser of productive services at present prices to convert into finished goods for sale at the prices prevailing when the operation is finished. There is no uncertainty as to the prices of the things he buys. He bears the technological uncertainty as to the amount

of physical product he will secure, but the probable error in calculations of this sort is generally not large; the gamble is in the price factor in relation to the product.

(Knight 1921, pp. 317–18)

Thus for Knight (as compared to Coase), output price uncertainty accounts for the unique nature of the firm. Transaction costs do not enter the picture at this stage of inquiry, because they are secondary to the originative acts of (1) deciding what goods are to be produced, and (2) establishing the appropriate administrative organization to do so. Whereas Coase took markets for granted, Knight wished to understand the dynamic problem of how markets are created. The creation of markets, he believed, is an entrepreneurial function. Prices allocate resources, but they do not create markets; entrepreneurs do. From Knight's perspective, therefore, the price system could never be viewed as a complete substitute for the entrepreneur.

Coase criticized Knight's theory because it neglected the role of contracts in defining entrepreneurial activity. However, we have seen that the chief function of Knight's entrepreneur is to contract away uncertainty by offering collateral guarantees (i.e., fixed payments) to resource suppliers. Ironically, Coase (1937, p. 347) found this element of contracting in Knight "irrelevant." What mattered most to him was finding the reason why the price mechanism should be superseded, and he could not discover this reason in Knight's treatment of the firm.

Coase's perceptive analysis of transaction costs eventually spawned a new literature that embellishes the idea of the entrepreneur as contractor.[3] The transactions-cost literature has flowered in contemporary microeconomic theory, thanks to Coase. Nevertheless, because he did not understand the true nature of Knight's inquiry, his criticisms of Knight were mostly misplaced. Coase advanced the analysis of the firm within a neoclassical framework that accepts the choice of product as given. He therefore assumed away the uncertainty that Knight openly confronted. Coase argued that firms emerge because of the costs of using the price mechanism – costs that can be reduced or avoided by bringing more internal transactions within a single administrative network. But as Boudreaux (1986, pp. 127–8) points out, this approach is more germane to questions of firm size (i.e., vertical integration) than to a theory of entrepreneurship.

Knight, like Schumpeter, was interested in explaining the nature of economic progress in a market system, the chief components of which are firms and entrepreneurs. By firm he meant a basic form of business organization in which the entrepreneur takes direction, control, and responsibility. Contracting alone does not capture the full role of the entrepreneur for Knight (1921, p. 353), because "In the world as it is the interests affected by contracts are never all represented in the agreements." In Knight's view, entrepreneurs are more than contractors. They are specialists at uncertainty-bearing, and while the contract is one way to reduce uncertainty, some uncertainty can never be eliminated. For Knight (1921, p. 283), therefore, the size of firms depends, among other things, upon the available supply of entrepreneurial qualities.

Is the firm the entrepreneur?

Knight's theory offered a balanced perspective on the functions of risk-taking and management. It set up a broad class of entrepreneurs because it did not limit the function of making provisional guaranties to the possessor(s) of the ownership equity in the firm. Indeed, one may have to move far up the management hierarchy in a Knightian firm in order to locate the function of ultimate control. Knight asserted that management's primary function is selection of people who make decisions required by the nature of the firm. The basic structure of the decision-making organization is a hierarchy of functionaries in which persons at each higher level select the functionaries below. Therefore, each functionary leaves the consequences of his activity to his selector, thereby continually shifting economic responsibility to a higher level, until it finally rests with the controlling functionaries (i.e., the guarantors of the contractual remunerations of resource suppliers). For Knight (1921, pp. 267–70, 276–7, 291–302) only this last decision is crucial; all subordinate decisions are routine and, consequently, non-entrepreneurial.

In a paper published in 1944, James H. Stauss argued that Knight's theory, although logically correct, is neither the only solution to the problem of entrepreneurial control nor the most relevant one. Stauss claimed that the facts of modern business deny the notion of a unique class having primacy in undertaking the functions of risk-taking and management. He proposed that the appropriate frame of reference for such undertakings is the firm. More specifically, he asserted that the firm is the entrepreneur (Stauss 1944, p. 112, 117, 120).

According to Stauss, the central problem in defining entrepreneurship is determination of the locus of control. He argued that Knight's entrepreneur is not unique because it is impossible to locate primacy in exercising the function of control formally in any one class of so-called 'entrepreneurs' grouped on the basis of some uniform relation to the firm, such as possession of the ownership equity or extension of provisional guaranties.

> The circumstances of time and place demand consideration in locating the controllers and deciding upon the importance of their decisions. Likewise, decision-making within jurisdictional spheres is in the face

of managerial problems of greater or less importance concerning the conduct of the firm. Cruciality of decisions is thus a relative matter.

(Stauss 1944, p. 118)

Stauss justified his view on the basis of two developments of modern enterprise that Knight neglected: (1) the rise of the corporation, in which the functions of ownership and decision-making were largely separated; and (2) the expansion of government regulation, which tended to blur distinctions between ownership, regulation, and administration. Because of these developments, he argued that ownership was less important as a central relation of entrepreneurship than the decision-making apparatus, which normally resides in the administrative structure of the firm. Even when the corporation is fully under private ownership, Stauss (1944, p. 119) maintained that "Other governmental agencies, and various authorities, may dominate the policies of the firm in many respects, possibly to the extent of governing the selection of hired executives."

Stauss claimed affinity with Schumpeter, whose overall economic framework he shared. This framework consists of an assembly of firms, supply functionaries, consumers, and government. According to Stauss, traditional theories of entrepreneurship (including Knight's) confuse the actions of supply functionaries and some managerial laborers with the actions of entrepreneurs. However, if the traditional perspective is reversed so that the firm is the entrepreneur, then, according to Stauss (1944, p. 121), "The functionaries introducing new [Schumpeterian] combinations would be, in the main, firms (old or new) acting through their aggregates of individual members with specified powers of decision." The new frame of reference would be competent to analyze the basic responsibilities of laborers to yield productive services and to initiate and continue relations with the firm, including the productive services of managers that are not entrepreneurs.

Although it is provocative to think of the firm as the entrepreneur, certain questions are raised by reversing the traditional concept of the entrepreneur operating through the medium of the firm. Ultimately, humans, not structures, make decisions; therefore we must resolve the question of what the firm is. Other questions also crowd in quickly. What is the difference between a firm and a bureaucracy? Does firm size affect the origination and implementation of decisions? In short, how does the view that the firm is the entrepreneur improve the theory of entrepreneurship?

Successful firms tend to grow, and larger firms tend to be dominated by rigid rules of conduct. The idea of the firm as the entrepreneur is likely to be opposed, therefore, on grounds of methodological individualism. Stauss (1944, p. 126) rejected the notion that the firm is a mere aggregation of decision-makers having a collective will expressed through a system of working rules. He proposed instead that the firm be treated as an accounting entity for purposes of general economic analysis and as a particular concrete institution when specific problems need to be solved. But he did not explain how to make this dual idea of the firm operational in economic theory, and after more than four decades, it is virtually impossible to find any trace of Stauss's influence on subsequent writers.

Postscript

The distinction between the entrepreneur and the firm, and the matter of their interchangeability, was seriously raised in the first half of the twentieth century. These matters remain unsettled among contemporary economists. Rather than meld the two into one entity, the sentiment seems to be to preserve a distinction, even if an ambiguous one, because the notion of personality apart from human beings is opposed in most quarters. Controversy on this subject has served to focus attention on the relation – symbiotic or otherwise – between the entrepreneur and the form of business organization within which he or she functions.

10 Conclusion

This book began with a taxonomy of who entrepreneurs are and what they do, according to how they have been exposited in economic literature. Now that we have concluded our historical survey, we can complete the taxonomy by associating certain writers with specific themes, mindful that significant overlap exists between writers and themes. To recapitulate, the various roles taken on by the entrepreneur in economics literature are:

1   The entrepreneur is the person who assumes the risk associated with uncertainty (Cantillon, von Thünen, von Mangoldt, Mill, Hawley, Knight, von Mises, Cole, Shackle).
2   The entrepreneur is the person who supplies financial capital (Smith, Turgot, von Böhm-Bawerk, Edgeworth, Pigou, von Mises).
3   The entrepreneur is an innovator (Baudeau, Bentham, von Thünen, Schmoller, Sombart, Weber, Schumpeter).
4   The entrepreneur is a decision-maker (Cantillon, Menger, Marshall, von Wieser, Amasa Walker, Francis Walker, Keynes, von Mises, Shackle, Cole, Schultz).
5   The entrepreneur is an industrial leader (Say, Saint-Simon, Amasa Walker, Francis Walker, Marshall, von Wieser, Sombart, Weber, Schumpeter).
6   The entrepreneur is a manager or superintendent (Say, Mill, Marshall, Menger).
7   The entrepreneur is an organizer and coordinator of economic resources (Say, Walras, von Wieser, Schmoller, Sombart, Weber, Clark, Davenport, Schumpeter, Coase).
8   The entrepreneur is the owner of an enterprise (Quesnay, von Wieser, Pigou, Hawley).
9   The entrepreneur is an employer of factors of production (e.g., Amasa Walker, Francis Walker, von Wieser, Keynes).
10   The entrepreneur is a contractor (Bentham).

11   The entrepreneur is an arbitrageur (Cantillon, Walras, Kirzner).

12   The entrepreneur is an allocator of resources among alternative uses (Cantillon, Kirzner, Schultz).

Our survey shows that throughout the ages theories of entrepreneurship have been both static and dynamic. However, upon reflection, it becomes obvious that only dynamic theories of entrepreneurship have any significant operational meaning. In a static world there is neither change nor uncertainty. The entrepreneur's role in a static state could not be anything more than what is implied above in item 2 (a supplier of financial capital), item 6 (a manager or superintendent), item 8 (the owner of an enterprise), or item 9 (an employer of factors of production). In a static world the entrepreneur is a passive element because his actions merely constitute repetitions of past procedures and techniques already learned and implemented. Only in a dynamic world does the entrepreneur become a robust figure. A dynamic environment is implied in each of the remaining definitions.

Once we have eliminated purely static representations of the subject, the taxonomy of entrepreneurial theories can be simplified by focusing on three major intellectual traditions, each spawned by Cantillon. For purposes merely of identification, let us call these three traditions the Chicago tradition (Knight–Schultz), the German tradition (von Thünen–Schumpeter), and the Austrian tradition (von Mises–Kirzner–Shackle).

This rather loose classification requires certain *obiter dicta*. To begin with, the lines of connection are not as straightforward as might be implied. Knight does not acknowledge Cantillon as the progenitor of his own theory of entrepreneurship, but the filiation of the two theories is too strong to ignore. Schultz (1980) openly aligns his theory with Knight's. The connection between von Thünen and Schumpeter, however, is tenuous, as is the connection between von Thünen and Cantillon. We base the linkage here more on convenience than historical fact. There is a certain logic to this connection insofar as von Thünen was the first to exposit the entrepreneur as an innovator in a language shared by Schumpeter. Of the connection between von Thünen and Cantillon, likewise, we have no direct evidence of linkage. There is no doubt, however, of the connection between von Mises and Kirzner.[1] Shackle appears as a parenthetical entry with the Austrians because his basic concept of the entrepreneur is Austrian, but he separates himself from them (and from other writers in this survey) by rejecting the equilibrium paradigm.

Despite its obvious oversimplifications, this classificatory scheme is useful for several purposes. For example, it provides a quick overview of the intellectual landscape. It emphasizes that those writers who most advanced the subject of the entrepreneur did so in the context of economic dynamics and the equilibrium paradigm.[2] Persistent themes in this literature emphasize perception, uncertainty, and innovation (or other special abilities). Some writers, such as Schumpeter, assert that the entrepreneur creates disequilibrium; while others, such as Kirzner, argue that he restores equilibrium after some exogenous shock. But this is a subtle difference that is of minor import to the overall understanding of the entrepreneurial function in a dynamic economy. Schumpeter certainly recognized the prevalence of other forces in the economy that work to restore equilibrium.

Another dominant trait of economics literature on the subject is that the entrepreneur should be defined according to function, not personality. However, Schumpeter (1954, pp. 896–7) cited two reasons why a functional theory might not capture all of the entrepreneurial gains or losses known to business practice. In the first place, the entrepreneur who stands between the commodity and factor markets is better placed to exploit favorable situations – to capture certain "leftovers" or residuals. In the second place, whatever their nature in other respects, practically speaking, entrepreneurs' gains will almost always bear some relation to monopolistic pricing.

We find the first of these arguments more compelling than the second, especially in view of Kirzner's (1973) attempt to clarify the distinction between competition and monopoly. By Kirzner's reasoning, true entrepreneurial gains have nothing to do with monopoly in its "proper" sense, which implies only that entry barriers exist. The problem of who has a legitimate claim to economic leftovers is, however, a thorny one that will, in our opinion, continue to plague the theory of entrepreneurship for some time to come.

An issue that has marred the historical treatment of entrepreneurship is whether the entrepreneur bears risk, uncertainty, or both. Early discussions made little or no distinction between risk and uncertainty, but all of that changed with the contribution of Frank Knight. Today there is growing consensus that non-entrepreneurial decision-making takes place under conditions of risk, whereas entrepreneurial decision-making takes place under conditions of uncertainty (cf. Alvarez and Busenitz 2001; Loasby 2002). The implications of this development will be discussed below.

Finally, contemporary economics continues to grapple with the proper relationship of the entrepreneur to the firm. In some instances the entrepreneur is seen as a substitute for the firm; in others he is seen as the progenitor and guiding hand of the firm; and in at least one instance it has been suggested that the entrepreneur *is* the firm.

Risk, uncertainty and organization

There is considerable appeal in the notion that everyone is a potential entrepreneur in one set of circumstances or another: the student, housewife, laborer, retiree, etc. who must deal with disequilibrating change (*à la* Shultz) or the people from any and all walks of life who are simply alert to opportunity (*à la* Kirzner). But economic discourse is dominated by the fact that entrepreneurs frequently organize firms in order to assemble and coordinate the economic resources required to exploit market opportunities.

Recently Sharon Alvarez and Jay Barney (2005) have argued that firms are established for different purposes. "Entrepreneurial firms are organized under conditions of uncertainty," they maintain, "and their primary purpose is to solve transaction difficulties associated with the inability to know the value of an exchange at the time that exchange is commenced." By contrast, non-entrepreneurial firms "are organized under conditions of risk, and their primary purpose is to solve transaction difficulties associated with allocating the value that a transaction is known to create among those that have made specific investments in an exchange" (2005, p. 788). Recognition of these different purposes, Alvarez and Barney contend, can not only help distinguish between types of firms but also help define the boundary of entrepreneurship as a research discipline.

The very fact that research boundaries are called for is a direct consequence of the fractured nature of the subject of entrepreneurship, which in turn is a consequence of its diverse historical evolution. Pursuit of the subject along the lines suggested by Alvarez and Barney requires that researchers concentrate not on the personality attributes of entrepreneurs that have been traditionally studied but rather on the distinction between risk and uncertainty introduced by Frank Knight. In the future, therefore, Knight may be more relevant to the subject of entrepreneurship than Schumpeter, at least among management specialists who study entrepreneurship.

Finding existing theories of how firms are organized inadequate,[3] Alvarez and Barney developed a typology of entrepreneurial firms that ranges from "clan-based" to "expert-based" to "charisma-based" organizations.[4] Decision-making in clan-based entrepreneurial firms is not hierarchical – with a boss telling others what to do – but democratic; its leaders tend to search for a consensus among all those who have made specific investments in the firm. As a result, clan-based entrepreneurial firms are characterized by a high degree of trust on the part of those involved in making transaction-specific investments. Expert-based entrepreneurial firms employ a somewhat traditional hierarchy, but the "boss" is chosen on the basis of his or her opportunity cost of joining the firm rather than on the basis of his or her ability to monitor and control. This "boss" is most likely to be someone having expert knowledge who is essential to the firm's success. Decision rights would be centered on this expert, who may make or delegate critical decisions. Charisma-based entrepreneurial firms are also hierarchical, but the "boss" exercising control operates on the basis of his or her charisma and vision rather than his or her specific expertise or ability to monitor and adjust incentives. If other firm members share the entrepreneur's vision, they give decision-making power to him or her. This "boss" would establish residual claims in the organization.

The broader issue confronted by Alvarez and Barney is that the distinction between risk and uncertainty helps to categorize entrepreneurial behavior. Under risk-based theories, it may be reasonable to think of opportunities as objective phenomena waiting to be discovered by entrepreneurs (Kirzner 1973; Shane 2003). But under uncertainty-based theories, entrepreneurs do not so much discover profit opportunities as create them, often through their organizing efforts (cf. Alvarez and Barney 2005, p. 788).

Among the ironies revealed by their research, Alvarez and Barney recognize that because the condition of uncertainty is often not stable over time, the bases of organizing entrepreneurial firms are not likely to be stable over time. In particular, uncertainty-based firms may turn into risk-based firms once the probability distribution of outcomes associated with uncertain exchanges is learned through experience. Entrepreneurial firms, in other words, may be temporary, but their persistence is nevertheless a prerequisite for the continual development of economic firms.

Past as prologue

It is difficult, if not impossible, to predict the future course of research on entrepreneurship. But several lessons can be learned from a study of the intellectual past. One lesson is that the place of entrepreneurship in economic theory is more a problem of method than a problem of theory. The history of economic theory clearly demonstrates that the entrepreneur was squeezed from economics when the discipline attempted to emulate the physical sciences by incorporating the mathematical method. Clearly mathematics brought greater precision to economics and thereby promised to increase its powers of prediction. Yet the introduction of mathematics to economics (about the time of Alfred Marshall) was a two-edged sword. Its sharp edge cut through a tangled confusion of real-world complexity, making economics more tractable and accelerating its theoretic advance. Its blunt edge, however, dulled one of the fundamental forces of economic life – the entrepreneur. Since there was not then, and is not now, a satisfactory mathematics to deal with the dynamics of economic life, economic analysis gradually receded into the shadows of comparative statics, and the entrepreneur took on a purely passive, even useless, role.

Another historical lesson is that, in its most fruitful phase, theorizing about entrepreneurship has been part of a broader search for the basic tenets of the dynamics of economic life. The dynamics of economic life involve relations between people as well as relations of people to material things. As economics became more like a branch of mechanics, it struck a kind of Faustian bargain in which its "soul" was sacrificed for a better glimpse of the future (i.e., prediction). Yet this future should have been suspect all along because the static method totally represses change. By contrast, dynamics *is* change, and, more than anything else, change is the province of the entrepreneur.

Does it matter whether the entrepreneur is the person who provokes change or merely adjusts to it? If we rely on the most elemental features of entrepreneurship – perception, courage, and action – the answer is, probably not. Entrepreneurial action means creation of opportunity as well as response to existing circumstances. Entrepreneurial action also implies that entrepreneurs have the courage to embrace risks in the face of uncertainty. The failure of perception, nerve, or action renders the entrepreneur ineffective. For this reason, we must look to these elements for the distinctive nature of the concept, not to the circumstances of action or reaction.

Just as theorizing about entrepreneurship has been most fruitful when economists have concerned themselves with the dynamics of economic life, so has it been least productive when economics has confined itself to the world of statics. At the close of our inquiry, therefore, we face the most basic of questions: What is the function of economics? Is it to enable us to understand the foundations of economic life or is it to predict the course of events that have yet to happen? If it is the former, we must take economic life as it is, with its imperfections, its risks, and its uncertainties. If it is the latter, we are justified in extruding from our theoretic models certain real-life conditions, but we must become aware of the costs of doing so.

We are finally confronted with the ultimate scientific dilemma. On the one hand, we can sacrifice realism to gain precision; on the other hand, we can give up precision to gain realism. The choice we make determines the place of the entrepreneur in economic theory. Ultimately, the reason the entrepreneur is such an important subject of economists' interest is because his or her function and character penetrate to the very core of economics and raise fundamental questions of economic method that have never been resolved – indeed, have not even been fully discussed in the economic light of day.

Notes

Introduction

1 See www.nationalconsortium.org. Of course, the topic of entrepreneurship has diffused through a number of disciplines besides business and economics.
2 Part of the increase in demand from students in the sciences and engineering fields is coming from the growth of student numbers in professional science master's degree programs. See www.sciencemasters.com.
3 Course topics range from history of economic thought to fostering an inventive business culture, and from buy-sell strategies to the functioning of venture capital markets.
4 In the many books that are now used as course material, the historical origin of the entrepreneur is generally noted to be Cantillon, but then the authors jump to Schumpeter, forgetting those scholars in between and forgetting that Schumpeter did not advance the notion of entrepreneurship as much as others had done.
5 The remainder of this book is structured around our earlier surveys (Hébert and Link 1988, 2006); however, over these past two decades our interpretation of many of the early writings has evolved, and we present that herein.

1 The prehistory of entrepreneurship

1 The same can be said in reverse; that is, the type of business organization can be tailored to the nature of entrepreneurial activity. On this point see Alvarez and Barney (2005).

2 Early French contributions

1 Knight's ideas on entrepreneurship are discussed in more detail in Chapter 6.
2 One French economist who took exception to Say's theory of entrepreneurship was Courcelle-Seneuil (1813–1892), who insisted that profit is not a wage but is due to the assumption of risk. Knight (1921, p. 25n) attributes to him a glimpse of "the fact that the assumption of a 'risk' of error in one's judgment, inherent in the making of a responsible decision, is a phenomenon of a different character from the assumption of 'risk' in the insurance sense."

3 The English school of thought

1 However, as late as 1931, in his English translation of Richard Cantillon's *Essai sur la Nature du Commerce en Général*, Henry Higgs replaced Cantillon's many references to "entrepreneur" with the word "undertaker," which imparts a decidedly anachronistic flavor for contemporary readers.

2 Pesciarelli (1989, p. 531) points out that four of the five new combinations that comprise innovation as emphasized by Schumpeter in his *Theory of Economic Development* (see Chapter 7) were previously identified by Bentham.

5 Early neoclassical perspectives

1 The meaning of this statement and its implications are not quite clear. A counterbalancing tendency between gains and losses might be posited in a long-run analysis where all "projects" are lumped together (cf. von Wieser 1927, p. 355). But from an individualist perspective, this assertion seems tantamount to the statement that each entrepreneurial opportunity has a 50–50 chance of success. Surely there is no a priori nor observed reason why this should be the case. In fact, Hawley and Clark later refuted this position (see Chapter 6).

2 In listing his criticisms of past writers, Walras's distinction between "English" and "French" was somewhat artificial: Turgot was guilty of the same "error" as the English classical economists (i.e., not separating capitalist and entrepreneur); and Mill was guilty of the same "error" as Say (i.e., identifying entrepreneurship with the coordination and supervision of productive factors).

3 The noted Swedish economist Knut Wicksell offered a similar criticism. Wicksell (1954 [1893], p. 95) claimed that Walras's entrepreneur is a mere fiction, because: (a) the buying of services and selling of goods in which he supposedly engages is more apparent than real (i.e., involves mere exchanges of productive services against each other), and (b) Walras completely overlooked the significance of time in production. Unhappily, in his own work Wicksell repeatedly blurred the distinctions between entrepreneur, landowner, capitalist, and worker.

4 In a parallel vein, Marshall made the simple declaration, "Knowledge is our most powerful engine of production" – an insight that is especially resonant in the digital age, which is often referred to as "the knowledge economy."

6 The view from America

1 Schumpeter (1954, p. 519) labeled Walker's *Science of Wealth* (1866) "a representative performance of the 'non-American' line of United States economics," alluding perhaps to the German influence mentioned above.

2 Compare with Cantillon's vision, as portrayed by Hoselitz (1960, p. 240), that the entrepreneur is someone who buys at a certain cost price and sells at an uncertain sales price.

3 On the deficiencies of the argument that the entrepreneur is a mere coordinator, see Hawley (1900, pp. 84–9).

4 To quote Fetter (1914, pp. 562–63) on Davenport: "Peruna, as an example of harmful yet valued products, is administered in large doses; and burglars with their jimmies, and loose women with their flaunting appeals, appear so often that they make some chapters of this book appear like an evening at the uncensored

movies." It is noteworthy that Irving Fisher, commenting on Davenport's earlier work, *Value and Distribution* (1908), recognized the "radical if not heretical" nature of that book but warmly praised its practical side and declared his hearty assent.

5 This same criticism had been leveled unsuccessfully against Walker by Macvane (1887, pp. 9–11). Taussig took no notice of Macvane's critique, nor of Walker's response (1888, p. 282).

7 Joseph Schumpeter

1 Mark W. Frank (1998) argues that failure to understand or appreciate Schumpeter's instrumentalist methodology has led to a misguided debate about the dichotomous nature of Schumpeter's entrepreneur. The alleged dichotomy is said to involve conflicting visions of the entrepreneur in Schumpeter's "European period" (1911–1931) versus his "American period" (1932–1950). In the former, Schumpeter characterized entrepreneurial innovation as the highly individualized actions of visionaries who create small, new firms; whereas in the latter (when he was preoccupied with the transformation of capitalism to socialism), Schumpeter made the exemplar entrepreneur much less individualistic, arguing that corporations and government agencies might assume the entrepreneurial mantle.

2 The idea of entrepreneurship as innovation has had practical applications as well as analytic impact. Gerry Sweeney (1985) contends that the goal of the Six Countries Programme of growth in Europe is to promote innovation by supporting entrepreneurship rather than other mechanisms of growth, such as research.

3 Brown and Atkinson (1981) express similar notions of the distribution of entrepreneurial talent on aspects of performance.

4 For a recent example, see Jonathan Hughes (1986).

8 Beyond Schumpeter

1 See also Karl W. Deutsch (1949), who outlined a functional analysis of the study of entrepreneurship resembling Cole's. Deutsch proposed that the analyst should identify the single most important technical or social function performed by the entrepreneur, then investigate the primary and secondary effects of this function with respect to a particular time and place.

2 Hugh G. J. Aitken (1949) stressed decision-making parameters in the entrepreneur's environment, such as advances in technical knowledge.

3 More recently, A. L. Minkes and G. R. Foxall (1980) and S. A. Alvarez and J. Barney (2005) have raised organizational issues in the study of entrepreneurship. Evans (1949), Spengler (1949), and Cole (1959) maintain that entrepreneurship is really a plural concept. Spengler has suggested that the entrepreneurial function can be conceived as a set of tasks that needs to be done and is done by an entrepreneurial group.

4 In addition to works cited by Schultz (1975), especially Wallace E. Huffman (1974), see also Edward B. Roberts and Herbert A. Wainer (1971), who conclude that in addition to education, a person's home and religious background have strong influences on goal orientation and motivation.

5 Von Mises (1949, pp. 248–9) defended the concept on methodological grounds: "There is no means of studying the complex phenomena of action other than first

to abstract from change altogether, then to introduce an isolated factor provoking change, and ultimately to analyze its effects under the assumption that other things remain equal."

6 Rothbard (1985, p. 282) argues that even the arbitrageur is subject to uncertainty: "The arbitrageur can perceive that a product sells for one price at one place and at a higher price somewhere else, and therefore buy in the first place to sell in the second. But he better be cautious. The transactions are not instantaneous, and something might occur in the interim to change the seemingly certain profits into losses. It is, after all, possible that the other entrepreneurs, far from purblind to the profit opportunity lying await for arbitrage, knew something which our would-be arbitrageur does not."

7 While admitting the analytical intractability of entrepreneurship, Baumol (1983) has endorsed the notion of a supply curve of entrepreneurial ability based on a number of exogenous influences (e.g., genetics, cultural conditions, educational systems, attitudes toward economic success, and so forth). In this regard, both Baumol and Schultz are squarely in the neoclassical tradition of economic theory.

8 Hostile antagonists of Leibenstein (e.g., Stigler 1976) question the very existence of the concept of X-inefficiency. More moderate critics assert that the "empty spaces" and "fuzzy areas" he attributes to production processes are characteristic of his theory as well.

9 The entrepreneur and the firm

1 Arrow (1974) and Williamson (1975), among others, have argued that the existence of economic organizations is evidence of market failure.

2 For a detailed analysis of these costs, and of the effect of cost differentials on firm size, see Donald J. Boudreaux (1986, pp. 18–30).

3 The classic reference to the "nexus of contracts" theory of the firm is Armen A. Alchian and Harold Demsetz (1972). See also Michale Jensen and William Meckling (1976), Paul Rubin (1978), and Benjamin Klein and Keith Leffler (1981). More recently, Yoram Barzel (1987) has used this approach to explore the moral hazard aspects of entrepreneurship. In a more fundamental historical sense, the idea of the entrepreneur as contractor harks back to Bentham.

10 Conclusion

1 Cantillon appears to have influenced the Austrians through Menger, whose personal library (now permanently residing at the Hitotsubashi University Library in Tokyo) contains a copy of Cantillon's *Essai sur la Nature du Commerce en Général*. We are grateful to Professor Chuhei Sugiyama for providing us with a catalog to the contents of the Menger Library.

2 Mark Blaug (1986, p. 230n) reminds us that two decades after the publication of his *Theory of Economic Development*, Schumpeter wrote a preface to the English translation in which he stated that the arguments of the book "might usefully be contrasted with the theory of [static] equilibrium, which explicitly or implicitly always has been and still is the center of traditional theory."

3 The two theories of how firms are organized that currently dominate the literature are transactions cost economics (Williamson 1975; 1985) and incomplete contract theory (Grossman and Hart 1986).

4 A basic premise of this approach is that whether a decision to invest in a market opportunity is risky or uncertain depends on the objective properties of that investment, not on the perceptions of decision-makers. "[N]o matter how a decision maker *feels* or what a decision maker *believes* or *perceives* about the outcomes of a decision, if the outcomes of a decision are not certain, then they are either risky or uncertain. If prior experience with that decision makes it possible to estimate a probability distribution associated with a decision, then that decision is risky. If it is not possible to estimate such a probability distribution, that decision is uncertain" (Alvarez and Barney 2005, p. 779).

References

Aitken, H. G. J. "The analysis of decisions," *Explorations in Entrepreneurial History*, vol. 1, pp. 17–23, 1949.

Alvarez, S. A. and J. B. Barney. "How do entrepreneurs organize firms under conditions of uncertainty," *Journal of Management*, vol. 31, pp. 776–93, 2005.

Alvarez, S. A. and L. Busenitz. "The entrepreneurship of resource-based theory," *Journal of Management*, vol. 27, pp. 755–75, 2001.

Alchian, A. A. and H. Demsetz. "Production, information costs, and economic organization," *American Economic Review*, vol. 62, pp. 777–95, 1972.

Aristotle. "The politics," translated by B. Jowett, in *Early Economic Thought*, edited by A. E. Monroe, Cambridge, MA: Harvard University Press, pp. 3–29, 1924.

Arrow, K. J. *The Limits of Organization*, New York: W. W. Norton, 1974.

Barzel, Y. "Knight's 'moral hazard' theory of organization," *Economic Inquiry*, vol. 25, pp. 117–20, 1987.

Baudeau, N. *Première Introduction à la Philosophie Économique*, edited by A. Dubois, Paris: P. Geuthner, 1910 [original 1767].

Baumol, W. J. "Entrepreneurship in economic theory," *American Economic Review, Papers and Proceedings*, vol. 58, pp. 64–71, 1968.

Baumol, W. J. "Towards operational models of entrepreneurship," in *Entrepreneurship*, edited by J. Ronen, Lexington, MA: D. C. Heath, pp. 29–48, 1983.

Bentham, J. *Jeremy Bentham's Economic Writings*, edited by W. Stark, London: Allen & Unwin, 1952.

Bentham, J. *The Works of Jeremy Bentham*, edited by J. Bowring, New York: Russell & Russell, 11 vols, 1962 [original 1838–43].

Bentham, J. 'Defense of Usary; shewing the impolicy of the present legal restraints on the terms of pecuniary bargains in a series of letters to a friend to which is added a letter to Adam Smith, Esq; LL.D. on the discouragements opposed by the above restraints to the progress of inventive industry", reprinted in W. Stark (ed.) *Jeremy Bentham's Economic Writings* 3 vols. (London: George Allen & Unwin), 1952, vol. 1, pp. 124–207, 1787.

Blaug, M. "Entrepreneurship before and after Schumpeter," in *Economic History and the History of Economics*, edited by M. Blaug, Brighton, England: Wheatsheaf Books, pp. 219–30, 1986.

Boudreaux, D. J. "Contracting, organization, and monetary instability: studies in the theory of the firm," Ph.D. dissertation, Auburn University, 1986.

Brown, D. J. and J. H. Atkinson, "Cash and share renting: an empirical test of the link between entrepreneurial ability and contractual choice," *Bell Journal of Economics*, vol. 12, pp. 296–9, 1981.

Cantillon, R. *Essai sur la Nature du Commerce en Général*, edited and translated by H. Higgs, London: Macmillan, 1931.

Carlin, E. A. "Schumpeter's constructed type – the entrepreneur," *Kyklos*, vol. 9, pp. 27–43, 1956.

Casson, M. "Entrepreneur," in *The New Palgrave: A Dictionary of Economics*, vol. 2, edited by J. Eatwell, M. Milgate, and P. Newman, London: Macmillan, p. 151, 1987.

Chandler, Jr., A. D. *Strategy and Structure*, Cambridge, MA: M.I.T. Press, 1962.

Clark, J. B. "Insurance and business profits," *Quarterly Journal of Economics*, vol. 7, pp. 45–54, 1892.

Clark, J. B. *Essentials of Economic Theory*, New York: Macmillan, 1907.

Coase, R. H. "The nature of the firm," *Economica*, N.S., vol. 4, pp. 386–405, 1937.

Cochran, T. C. "Entrepreneurship," in *International Encyclopedia of the Social Sciences*, edited by David L. Sills, New York: Macmillan, pp. 87–91, 1968.

Cole, A. H. "An approach to the study of entrepreneurship: a tribute to Edwin F. Gay," *Journal of Economic History*, vol. 6, pp. 1–15, 1946.

Cole, A. H. "Entrepreneurship and entrepreneurial history," in *Change and the Entrepreneur*, prepared by the Research Center in Entrepreneurial History, Cambridge, MA: Harvard University Press, pp. 85–107, 1949.

Cole, A. H. *Business Enterprise in its Social Setting*, Cambridge, MA: Harvard University Press, 1959.

Davenport, H. *Value and Distribution*, New York: Augustus M. Kelley, 1908 [reprinted 1964].

Davenport, H. *The Economics of Enterprise*, New York: Macmillan, 1913.

De Roover, R. "The organization of trade,"in *The Cambridge Economic History of Europe*, vol. 3: Economic Organization and Policies in the Middle Ages, M. M. Postan, ed. Cambridge, UK: Cambridge University Press, pp. 49–50, 1963.

Destutt de Tracy, A. L. C. *A Treatise on Political Economy*, translated by Thomas Jefferson, New York: Augustus M. Kelley, 1970 [original 1817].

Deutsch, K. W. "A note on the history of entrepreneurship, innovation and decision-making," *Explorations in Entrepreneurial History*, vol. 1, pp. 8–12, 1949.

Dobb, M. "Entrepreneur," in *Encyclopedia of the Social Sciences*, edited by E. R. A. Seligman, New York: Macmillan, pp. 558–60, 1937.

Edgeworth, F. Y. "Application of the differential calculus to economics," in Edgeworth, F.Y., *Papers Relating to Political Economy*, 3 vols. New York: Burt Franklin, pp. 367–82, 1925.

Evans, Jr., G. H. "The entrepreneur and economic theory: an historical and analytical approach," *American Economic Review*, vol. 39, pp. 336–55, 1949.

Fetter, F. A. "Davenport's competitive economics," *Journal of Political Economy*, vol. 22, pp. 550–65, 1914.

Forrester, J. W. "A new corporate design," *Industrial Management Review*, vol. 7, pp. 5–18, 1965.

Frank, M. W. "Schumpeter on entrepreneurs and innovation: a reappraisal," *Journal of the History of Economic Thought*, vol. 20, pp. 505–16, 1998.

Galbraith, J. K. *The New Industrial State*, Boston: Houghton Mifflin, 1967.

Gay, E. F. "The rhythm of history," *Harvard Graduates' Magazine*, vol. 32, pp. 1–16, 1923–24.

Grossman, S. and O. Hart. "The costs and benefits of ownership: a theory of vertical and lateral integration," *Journal of Political Economy*, vol. 94, pp. 691–719, 1986.

Halévy, É. *The Growth of Philosophic Radicalism*, translated by Mary Morris, Boston: Beacon Press, 1955.

Harbison, F. "Entrepreneurial organization as a factor in economic development," *Quarterly Journal of Economics*, vol. 70, pp. 364–79, 1956.

Hawley, F. B. "The fundamental error of Kapital and Kapitalzins," *Quarterly Journal of Economics*, vol. 6, pp. 280–307, 1892.

Hawley, F. B. "The risk theory of profit," *Quarterly Journal of Economics*, vol. 7, pp. 459–79, 1893.

Hawley, F. B. "Enterprise and profit," *Quarterly Journal of Economics*, vol. 15, pp. 75–105, 1900.

Hébert, R. F. "Was Richard Cantillon an Austrian economist?" *Journal of Libertarian Studies*, vol. 7, pp. 269–79, 1985.

Hébert, R. F. and A. N. Link. *The Entrepreneur: Mainstream Views and Radical Critiques*, New York: Praeger, 1982, 2nd edition 1988.

Hébert, R. F. and A. N. Link. "Historical perspectives on the entrepreneur," *Foundation and Trends in Entrepreneurship*, vol. 2, pp. 261–408, 2006.

Hennings, K. H. "The transition from classical to neoclassical economic theory: Hans von Mangoldt," *Kyklos*, vol. 33, pp. 658–82, 1980.

Hermann, F. D. W. *Staatswirtschaftliche Untersuchungen Über Vermögen, Wirthschaft, Produktivitat der Arbeiten, Kapital, Preis, Gewinn, Einkommen und Verbrauch*, Munich: A. Weber, 1832.

Hirschman, A. O. *The Strategy of Economic Development*, New Haven, CT: Yale University Press, 1958.

Hoselitz, B. F. "The early history of entrepreneurial theory," in *Essays in Economic Thought: Aristotle to Marshall*, edited by J. J. Spengler and W. R. Allen, Chicago: Rand McNally, pp. 235–57, 1960.

Hufeland, G. *Neue Grundlegung der Staatswirthschaftskunst*, Vienna: B. P. Bauer, 1815.

Huffman, W. E. "Decision making: the role of education," *American Journal of Agricultural Economics*, vol. 56, pp. 85–97, 1974.

Hughes, J. *The Vital Few: The Entrepreneur and American Economic Progress*, Oxford: Oxford University Press, 1986.

Hutchison, T. W. *A Review of Economic Doctrines, 1870–1929*, Oxford: Clarendon Press, 1953.

Jaffé, W. "Walras' economics as others see it," *Journal of Economic Literature*, vol. 18, pp. 528–49, 1980.

Jenks, L. H. "Role structure of entrepreneurial personality," in *Change and the Entrepreneur*, prepared by the Research Center in Entrepreneurial History, Cambridge, MA: Harvard University Press, pp. 108–52, 1949.

Jensen, M. and W. Meckling. "The theory of the firm: managerial behavior, agency costs and ownership structure," *Journal of Financial Economics*, vol. 3, pp. 305–60, 1976.

Kanbur, S. M. "Of risk taking and the personal distribution of income," *Journal of Political Economy*, vol. 87, pp. 769–97, 1979.

Kanbur, S. M. "A note on risk taking, entrepreneurship, and Schumpeter," *History of Political Economy*, vol. 12, no. 4, pp. 489–98, 1980.

Katz, J. A. "A chronology and intellectual trajectory of American entrepreneurship education: 1876–1999," *Journal of Business Venturing*, vol. 18, pp. 283–300, 2003.

Keynes, J. M. *The General Theory of Employment, Interest, and Money*, New York: Harcourt, Brace and World, 1964.

Kirzner, I. M. *Competition and Entrepreneurship*, Chicago: University of Chicago Press, 1973.

Kirzner, I. M. *Perception, Opportunity, and Profit: Studies in the Theory of Entrepreneurship*, Chicago: University of Chicago Press, 1979a.

Kirzner, I. M. "Comment: X-inefficiency, error, and the scope for entrepreneurship," in *Time, Uncertainty and Disequilibrium*, edited by M. Rizzo. Lexington, MA: D. C. Heath, pp. 140–51, 1979b.

Kirzner, I. M. *Discovery and the Capitalist Process*, Chicago: University of Chicago Press, 1985.

Klein, B. and K. Leffler. "The role of market forces in assuring contractual performance," *Journal of Political Economy*, vol. 89, pp. 615–41, 1981.

Knight, F. H. *Risk, Uncertainty and Profit*, New York: Houghton Mifflin, 1921.

Knight, F. H. *The Economic Organization*, New York: Augustus M. Kelley, 1951.

Lane, F. C. "Recent studies on the economic history of Venice," *Journal of Economic History*, vol. 23, pp. 312–34, 1963.

Leibenstein, H. "Entrepreneurship and development," *American Economic Review*, vol. 48, pp. 72–83, 1968.

Leibenstein, H. "The general X-efficiency paradigm and the role of the entrepreneur," in *Time, Uncertainty and Disequilibrium*, edited by M. Rizzo, Lexington, MA: D. C. Heath, pp. 127–39, 1979.

Link, A. N. and J. R. Link. *Government as Entrepreneur*, Oxford: Oxford University Press, 2009.

Loasby, B. "The organizational basis of cognition and the cognitive basis of organization," in *The Economics of Choice, Change and Organization: Books in Honor of Richard M. Cyert*, edited by M. Augier and J. G. March, Cheltenham, England: Edward Elgar, pp. 147–67, 2002.

Macdonald, R. "Schumpeter and Max Weber: central visions and social theories," in *Entrepreneurship and Economic Development*, edited by P. Kilby, New York: Free Press, 1971.

Machlup, F. *Knowledge and Knowledge Production*, Princeton, NJ: Princeton University Press, 1980.

Macvane, S. M. "Business profits," *Quarterly Journal of Economics*, vol. 2, pp. 1–36, 1887.

Maidique, M. A. "Entrepreneurs, champions, and technological innovation," *Sloan Management Review*, vol. 21, pp. 59–76, 1980.

Malmgren, H. B. "Information, expectations and the theory of the firm," *Quarterly Journal of Economics*, vol. 75, pp. 399–421, 1961.

Mangoldt, H. von. "The precise function of the entrepreneur and the true nature of entrepreneur's profit," in *Some Readings in Economics*, edited by F. M. Taylor, Ann Arbor, MI: George Wahr, pp. 34–49, 1907 [original 1855].

Marshall, A. *Principles of Economics*, 8th edition, London: Macmillan, 1920a.

Marshall, A. *Industry and Trade*, 3rd edition, London: Macmillan, 1920b.

Marshall, A. *Memorials of Alfred Marshall*, edited by A. C. Pigou, London: Macmillan, 1925.

Mason, E. S. "Saint-Simonism and the rationalisation of industry," *Quarterly Journal of Economics*, vol. 45, pp. 640–83, 1931.

Meek, R. L. *Turgot on Progress, Sociology and Economics*, Cambridge: Cambridge University Press, 1973.

Menger, C. *Principles of Economics*, translated by J. Dingwall and B. F. Hoselitz, Glencoe, IL: Free Press, 1950 [original 1871].

Mill, J. S. *Principles of Political Economy*, edited by W. J. Ashley, New York: Augustus M. Kelley, 1965 [original 1848].

Minkes, A. L. and G. R. Foxall. "Entrepreneurship, strategy, and organization: individual and organization in the behavior of the firm," *Strategic Management Journal*, vol. 1, pp. 295–301, 1980.

Mises, L. von. *Human Action: A Treatise on Economics*, New Haven, CT: Yale University Press, 1949.

Mises, L. von. *Profit and Loss*, South Holland, IL: Consumers-Producers Economic Service, 1951.

Morishima, M. *Walras' Economics: A Pure Theory of Capital and Money*, Cambridge: Cambridge University Press, 1977.

Papandreou, A. G. "The location and scope of the entrepreneurial function," Ph.D. dissertation, Harvard University, 1943.

Penrose, E. *The Theory of the Growth of the Firm*, New York: John Wiley and Sons, 1959.

Pesciarelli, E. "Smith, Bentham and the development of contrasting ideas on entrepreneurship," *History of Political Economy*, vol. 21, pp. 521–36, 1989.

Pigou, A. C. *Industrial Fluctuations*, 2nd edition, London: Macmillan, 1929.

Pigou, A. C. *Employment and Equilibrium*, 2nd edition, London: Macmillan, 1949.

Plant, A. "Centralise or decentralise?" Originally published in *Some Modern Business Problems*, ed. A. Plant, New York, Longmans, 1937. Reprinted in *Selected Economic Books and Addresses*, London, Routeledge and Kegan Paul, pp. 178–98, 1974.

Postlethwayt, Malachy *The University dictionary of trade and commerce, translated from the French of the celbrated monsieur Savary: with large additions and improvements, incorporated throughout the whole work; which more particularly accomodate the same to the trade and navigation of these kingdoms, and the laws, customs, and usages, to which all traders are subject.* 2 vols. London: John and Paul Knapton, 1751–55.

Quesnay, F. *Oeuvres Economiques et Philosophiques*, edited by A. Oncken, Frankfurt: M. J. Baer, 1888.

Rectenwald, H. C. "Mangoldt, Hans Karl Emil von," in *The New Palgrave: A Dictionary of Economics*, vol. 3, edited by J. Eatwell, M. Milgate, and P. Newman, London: Macmillan, p. 299, 1987.

Redlich, F. "Towards a better theory of risk," *Explorations in Entrepreneurial History*, vol. 10, pp. 33–9, 1957.

Redlich, F. "Toward the understanding of an unfortunate legacy," *Kyklos*, vol. 19, pp. 709–16, 1966.

Ricardo, David *On the Principles of Political Economy and Taxation*, reprinted in Piero Sraffa, ed., *The Works and Correspondence of David Ricardo*, vol. 1, Cambridge, UK: Cambridge University Press, 1996 [original 1819].

Riedel, A. F. J. *Nationalokonomie oder Volkswirthschaft Dargestellt*, 3 vols, Berlin: F. H. Morin, 1838–42.

Roberts, E. B. and H. A. Wainer. "Some characteristics of technical entrepreneurs," *IEEE Transactions on Engineering Management*, vol. EM-18, pp. 100–9, 1971.

Roscher, W. G. F. (1854) *Die Gundlagen der Nationalökonomie*, translated from 13th editon by J.J. Lalor as *Principles of Political Economy*, 2 vols., New York, 1878.

Roover, R. de. "The organization of trade," in *The Cambridge Economic History of Europe*, vol. 3, pp. 49–50, 1963a.

Roover, R. de. "The scholastic attitude toward trade and entrepreneurship," *Explorations in Entrepreneurial History*, vol. 3, pp. 76–87, 1963b.

Rothbard, M. N. "Professor Hébert on entrepreneurship," *Journal of Libertarian Studies*, vol. 7, pp. 281–6, 1985.

Rubin, P. "The theory of the firm and the structure of the franchise contract," *Journal of Law and Economics*, vol. 21, pp. 223–33, 1978.

Say, J. B. *Cours Complet d'Économie Politique Pratique*, 2nd edition, Paris: Guillaumin. 2 vols, 1840 [original 1828–29].

Say, J. B. *A Treatise on Political Economy*, 4th edition, translated by C. R. Prinsep, Philadelphia: Grigg & Elliot, 1845 [original 1803].

Savary des Bruslons, Jacques. *Dictionnaire Universel de Commerce:* contenant tout ce qui concerne le commerce qui se fait dans les quatre parties du monde. 2 vols. Paris: Jacques Estienne, 1723.

Schön, D. A. "Champions for radical new inventions," *Harvard Business Review*, vol. 2, pp. 77–86, 1963.

Schön, D. A. *Technology and Change: The New Heraclitus*, New York: Delacorte Press, 1976.

Schultz, T. W. "The value of the ability to deal with disequilibria," *Journal of Economic Literature*, vol. 13, pp. 827–46, 1975.

Schultz, T. W. "Investment in entrepreneurial ability," *Scandinavian Journal of Economics*, vol. 82, pp. 437–48, 1980.

Schumpeter, J. A. "The instability of capitalism," *Economic Journal*, vol. 38, pp. 361–86, 1928.

Schumpeter, J. A. *The Theory of Economic Development*, translated by R. Opie from the 2nd German edition [1926], Cambridge: Harvard University Press, 1934 [original 1912].

Schumpeter, J. A. *Business Cycles*, New York: McGraw-Hill, 1939.

Schumpeter, J. A. *Capitalism, Socialism and Democracy*, 3rd edition, New York: Harper & Row, 1950.

Schumpeter, J. A. *History of Economic Analysis*, edited by E. B. Schumpeter, New York: Oxford University Press, 1954.

Shackle, G. L. S. *Uncertainty in Economics*, Cambridge: Cambridge University Press, 1955.

Shackle, G. L. S. *The Nature of Economic Thought*, Cambridge: Cambridge University Press, 1966.

Shane, S. *A General Theory of Entrepreneurship: The Individual-Opportunity Nexus*. Cheltenham, UK: Edward Elgar Publishing, 2003.

Shove, G. F. "The place of Marshall's 'Principles' in the development of economic theory," *Economic Journal*, vol. 52, pp. 294–329, 1942.

Smith, A. *The Theory of Moral Sentiments*, edited by D. D. Raphael and A. L. Macfie, vol. 1 of the Glasgow Edition of the *Works and Correspondence of Adam Smith* (7 vols), Oxford: Oxford University Press, 1976a [original 1759].

Smith, A. *An Inquiry into the Nature and Causes of the Wealth of Nations*, edited by R. A. Campbell and A. S. Skinner, vol 2 of the Glasgow Edition of the *Works and Correspondence of Adam Smtih* (7 vols), Oxford: Oxford University Press, 1976b [original 1776].

Spengler, J. J. Discussion to "Possibilities for a realistic theory of entrepreneurship," *American Economic Review*, vol. 39, pp. 352–6, 1949.

Spengler, J. J. "Adam Smith's theory of economic growth Part II," *Southern Economic Journal*, vol. 26, pp. 1–12, 1959.

Spengler, J. J. and W. R. Allen, editors. *Books in Economic Thought: Aristotle to Marshall*, Chicago: Rand McNally, 1960.

Stauss, J. H. "The entrepreneur: the firm," *Journal of Political Economy*, vol. 52, pp. 112–27, 1944.

Stigler, G. J. "The xistence of x-efficiency," *American Economic Review*, vol. 66, pp. 213–16, 1976.

Sweeney, G. "Innovation is entrepreneur-led," in *Innovation Policies: An International Perspective*, edited by G. Sweeney, New York: St. Martin's Press, pp. 80–113, 1985.

Taussig, F. W. *Principles of Economics*, revised edition, vol. 2, New York: Macmillan, 1915.

Thünen, J. H. von. "The isolated state in relation to agriculture and political economy," vol. 2 [1850], translated by B. W. Dempsey and reprinted in B. W. Dempsey, *The Frontier Wage*, by B. W. Dempsey, Chicago: Loyola University Press, pp. 187–368, 1960.

Turgot, A. R. J. *The Economics of A. R. J. Turgot*, edited and translated by P. D. Groenewegen, The Hague: Martinus Nijhoff, 1977.

Turgot, A. R. J. *Reflections on the Formation and Distribution of Wealth* (1766). In P.D. Groenewegen (ed.) *The Economics of A. R. J. Turgot* (The Hague: Martinus Nijhoff, 1977), pp. 43–95.

Tuttle, C. A. "The entrepreneur function in economic literature," *Journal of Political Economy*, vol. 35, pp. 501–21, 1927.

Walker, A. *The Science of Wealth*, Boston: Little, Brown, 1866.

Walker, D. "Walras' theory of the entrepreneur," *De Economist*, vol. 134, pp. 1–24, 1986.

Walker, F. A. *The Wages Question*, New York: Henry Holt, 1876.

Walker, F. A. *Political Economy*, New York: Henry Holt, 1884.

Walker, F. A. "The source of business profits," *Quarterly Journal of Economics*, vol. 1, pp. 265–88, 1887.

Walker, F. A. "A reply to Mr Macvane: on the source of business profits," *Quarterly Journal of Economics*, vol. 2, pp. 263–96, 1888.

Walras, L. *Elements of Pure Economics*, translated by W. Jaffe, Homewood, IL: Richard D. Irwin, Inc, 1954 [original 1874].

Walras, L. *Correspondence of Leon Walras and Related Papers*, 3 vols, edited by W. Jaffe, Amsterdam: North-Holland Press, 1965.

Weber, M. *The Protestant Ethic and the Spirit of Capitalism*, translated by Talcott Parsons, New York: Scribner's, 1930.

White, L. H. "Entrepreneurship, imagination and the question of equilibration," Unpublished manuscript, 1976.

Wicksell, K. *Value, Capital and Rent*, English translation, London: George Allen & Unwin, 1954 [original 1893].

Wieser, F. von. *Social Economics*, translated by A. F. Hindrichs, New York: Adelphi, 1927.

Williamson, O. E. *Markets and Hierarchies*, New York: The Free Press, 1975.

Williamson, O. E. *The Economic Institutions of Capitalism*, New York: The Free Press, 1985.

Zrinyi, J. "Entrepreneurial behavior in economic theory: an historical and analytical approach," Ph.D. dissertation, Georgetown University, 1962.

Index of Names

	DATE DUE		